Sacred Angel Realms
A Pocket Guide into Nine Angelic Hierarchies

Angel Lady Terrie Marie, D.Ms.

OTHER PRODUCTS
by Angel Lady Terrie Marie, D.Ms.

BOOKS

Crystals and Minerals: Metaphysical Properties Easy Reference Guide
Angels Have Messages for You: 7 Secrets to Hear, Connect and Communicate with Angels
Inner Balance and Harmony: Angel Messages for Healing and Inspiration
Spiritual Expansion: 6 Ways to Expand Your Awareness
Crystal Grids: How to Make and Activate Crystal Grids
Element Angels: Expand Your Conscious Awareness

AUDIO PROGRAMS and MEDITATION CDs

Manifest with Angels: Focus Your Intentions
Earth Mother to Sky Father Chakra Alignment
Connecting with Angels: How to Receive Guidance and Messages from Angels
You, Your Energy and Money! The Friendly Side of Money

SELF-STUDY COURSES

Guardian Angels On Call: How to Create Your Personal 24/7 Relationship
Divine Magic: Nine Sacred Secrets to Divine Wealth
How to Create Your Ultimate Angel Dream Team

MISCELLANEOUS

Wings of Spirit Angel Cards (44 card-set)

Love and Romance Angel Cards (5 card-set)
Chakra Angel Cards (9 card-set)
Archangel Cards (5 card-set)

All of the above may be ordered by visiting:
http://www.angeldreamteam.com/
or through Angel Lady Terrie Marie, D. Ms. At
TerrieMarie@AngelDreamTeam.com

CONTENTS

    Page

Part One: the Heaven of Form
Chapter 1: Guardian Angels   4
Chapter 2: Archangels   16
Chapter 3: Angel Princes   27

Part Two: the Heaven of Creation
Chapter 4: Angels of the Powers   37
Chapter 5: Angels of the Virtues   47
Chapter 6: Angels of the Dominions   59

Part Three: the Heaven of Paradise
Chapter 7: Angels of the Thrones   73
Chapter 8: Angels of the Cherubim   81
Chapter 9: Angels of the Seraphim   88

Copyright © 2015 Angel Lady Terrie Marie, D.Ms. All rights reserved. No part of this publication may be reproduced or transmitted in any form or by any means, electronic or mechanical, including photocopying without written permission of the Publisher. Any unauthorized use, sharing, reproduction, or distribution is strictly prohibited. It is illegal to copy this book, post it to a website, or distribute it by any other means without permission from the Publisher.

Cover Design and Angel Artwork by Israel, Tovar Printing; El Paso, Texas

Distributed by
Angel Lady Aurora, LLC
El Paso, Texas Unites States
© 2015 – All Rights Reserved WorldWide

Limits of Liability and Disclaimer of Warranty

The Author and Publisher shall not be liable for your misuse of this material. This book is strictly for informational and educational purposes only.

Disclaimer

The purpose of this book is to educate and entertain. The Author and/or Publisher do not guarantee that anyone following these techniques, suggestions, tips ideas or strategies will become successful. The Author and/or Publisher shall have neither liability nor responsibility to anyone with respect to any loss or damage caused, or alleged to be caused, directly or indirectly by the information contained in this book.

Dedicated to ~
My Family and Friends for your unwavering support and encouragement
Students and Clients for giving me the gift of sharing my knowledge and experiences with you
LightWorkers and Healers I have met along the way
Mentors, Teachers and Coaches who have helped me stand in my truth of who I am and what I came here to do ...
and to
my beloved Angels and Divine Source
~ Angel Lady Terrie Marie, D.Ms.

The Angels Lady's Mission Statement: Help as many women and men as possible to connect with their Angels and live their Life Purpose with prosperity and abundance.

Preface

This is the story of how Sacred Angel Realms came to be. It would take me on an inner-journey unlike any other... join me for what will be an unforgettable journey among Angels ...

If you have been a part of my online community for a while, or if this is the first time we are connecting ... from my heart to your heart, it is a pleasure and an honor to be sharing the journey with you.

At the time of writing this writing, the first three chapters are now complete and true to form, my Angels are guiding me to share the story of how this unassuming, yet powerful book came to be.

The idea was first given to me in July or August of 2014. I was already working on two other major projects --- *Divine Magic: Nine Sacred Secrets of Divine Wealth* and Conversations with Angels: Raise Your Inner Vibration Mentally and Emotionally, the first of what will be a series of Conversation with Angels books.

What felt like being in the middle of working on my own Spiritual Journey, growing my business and working with more clients than ever before, in *floats* this guidance ... we want you to write a book about us.

The conversation with my Angels went something like this ...

"(Angels) Child we want you to write a book about us.
(Me) Isn't that what we are already working on?
(Angels) No, we want you to write about us.
(Me) Can you be more specific, help me understand you?
(Angels) Yes, write about our realms.
(Me) You want me to write a book, an in-depth, detailed book about all nine Angelic Realms?
(Angels) Yes, this is what we require of you now.
(Me) I have no idea how I am going to do this, there isn't very much information about this.
(Angels) Yes, this is why we come to you to tell our story.

(Me) Okay, but I first have to finish Divine Magic.
(Angels) Agreed. This is acceptable.
(Me) Just to be clear, after Divine Magic is complete and that is still 5 to 6 months from now, your guidance is for me to start on a book about you and all nine realms.
(Angels) Yes.
(ME) What is the title?
(Angels) This we give you --- Sacred Angel Realms: A Pocket Guide into Nine Angelic Realms. (Me) Okay."

    I remember my head starting to swim. The task I agreed to felt incredibly overwhelming. I went into my garden to ground and wrap my conscious-mind around this new guidance. I had just gotten used to the idea of channeling actual conversations with Angels. So I took lots of deep breaths and got busy finishing Divine Magic.

    It was time to start and I found myself procrastinating because I had no idea how I was going to be able to channel information about seven of the nine Angelic Realms ... I didn't even know the names of all of them by heart yet! This was definitely an OMG moment!

    At first I thought I was going to be starting at the top with the Seraphim Angels. I admit, I wasn't ready to do that. It felt rather overwhelming. Again I "asked" for help and support from my Angels and I was guided to start with Guardian Angels and then Archangels, both of whom I have been doing extensive work with for nearly 13 years. Okay, I could do that.

    The next step was starting with an introduction for the first chapter about Guardian Angels. When channeling the introduction, I realized I was being given an "Angelic Realm Map" and all I had to do was follow the guidance as it was being given to me for each of the Nine Sacred Angelic Realms what would become chapters. Okay, I can do that.

    So, the first two chapters were a stretch for me and in other ways, I found it to be very familiar. When it came time to start Chapter Three on Angel Princes, there was some resistance ... I wasn't sure I could really do this. Again I "asked" for guidance. I was gently guided to use three Angel books as a starting point. This enabled me to tap into the energetic-vibration of each one of the Angelic Realms, and be open to receive the information for the introduction.

Once I understood just how closely we --- the Angels and I --- were beginning to work together, it was much easier. Oh, just to be clear ... I am not saying it was obstacle free. I still got to up-level my own inner-vibration each step of the way so I could be a clear and perfect channel for all that was and would continue to come through me for you and everyone who reads these pages.

In the end, I didn't write an entire book. I wrote and channeled one chapter at a time. Each chapter was written and channeled one section at a time. Sometimes a single chapter would take two or three months to complete.

Channeling this book has taken me on an inner-journey unlike any other. Every word was first written by hand, in pencil in a special rose colored notebook. Then I would transcribe my own notes usually within 24 to 48 hours.

It has been a humbling experience to set my human self aside, allowing the energy to flow through me for you, to help you connect with Angels as you take your journey through each one of these nine Angelic Realms.

Enjoy the journey beautiful Souls of Light and Love!

Much Love, Light and Prosperity,
Angel Lady Terrie Marie, D.Ms.

Part One: the Heaven of Form
Guardian Angels
Archangels
Angel Princes

Part One: The Heaven of Form
An Introduction to Guardian Angels, Archangels, and Angel Princes

Angels of the Heaven of Form are in the Angelic realm closest to humankind energetically. Their energy is the easiest for us to sense, see, feel and connect with. It is easy for us to lift or draw back the veil that separates this Angelic Realm from our own dense physical energy. There is a specific level of consciousness that enables us to connect with all Angels, especially Angels charged with guiding and protecting all life on this planet.

One of the many gifts Angels of the Heaven of Form have for us, is the ability to transcend the ordinary everyday issues that seem to consume most of our waking moments. Being able to rise above obstacles, fear and doubt, pain and suffering is absolutely essential in connecting with Angels and raising our inner-vibration to truly get clarity about who we are and what we came here to do.

Every person and thing has a Spark of Divinity, deep within our heart-center. The Spark of Divinity, also known as the Divine Flame, connects us with each other, to Mother Earth and to the Stars in the heavens above. Being willing to see and accept that everyone and everything is a Divine Being in their own right, regardless of outward appearances to the contrary, is actually giving yourself the gift of seeing the Spark of Divinity within you.

The first, or closest to us energetically, are Guardian Angels whose primary responsibility is to nurture, love, guide and protect the human child who then becomes awakened, or remains in a state of perpetual sleepwalking. They assist us with Spiritual Growth, retaining lessons learned and seeing through self-imposed limitations, keeping us small and feeling unfulfilled.

Guardian Angels work hand-in-hand with Archangels as messengers of Divine Source, and they are gifted with being in all places in any given moment.

Archangels are able to transcend the limitations of time and space as we know and understand it. It is their ability to move about the heavens as they please, that gifts us all with their amazing healing energy. Archangels can be subtle. They can also be in *your face* if we fail to heed their signs, messages and guidance.

The highest vibrating Angels in this Angelic Realm are the Angel Princes, protectors and guardians of rulers and leaders in all walks of life. Their primary task is to influence all of us with compassion for ourselves and each other. It's also about making decisions from our heart-center, balancing mental and emotional energy, tempering Ego-based decisions.

Angel Princes represent the collective unconscious of humanity, encompassing the four elements of thought, emotion, energy and intuition.

Some of what is being shared with you in these pages will be familiar, while the rest will stretch your current level of understanding about Angels. All that is being asked of you is to have an open mind and an open heart.

Chapter One: Guardian Angels

What are Guardian Angels, what is their function and how many do you have, are just a few of the many questions men and women just like you have. So let's start at the very beginning and I'll share with you my understanding of what and who Guardian Angels are and how many you have with you.

The moment you are conceived is the moment your Guardian Angels are with you. These special Emissaries of the Angelic Realm agree to be with you for your entire life. Many times, the same Guardian Angels will be with you through your many lifetimes because these special messenger Angels stay with the same Soul throughout its journey.

Every person has at least two Guardian Angels with them at all times. Some people have more than two, but everyone has at least two.

There are many lessons and experiences that are learned and remembered. Some people believe we make agreements, Soul Agreements or Contracts to learn certain things, meet specific types of people and have particular experiences.

I am often asked how many Angels someone has around them. The total number of Angels with you at any given moment varies and depends on what is happening, if you have asked for help or need comfort and healing.

A person who works with Angels or asks for Angels to be with them, have more Angels than most people do simply because they ask for many Angels to be with them. It is very simple to ask. All you need to do is say --- Angels please come be with me --- the next step is then being open to accepting that your request has been heard and then answered.

Angels aren't allowed to interfere in your life for any reason and you must ask them for their help. The one and only time an Angel is allowed to interfere is if your life is in grave danger and it's not your time to leave or transition from this life to the next.

Guardian Angels on the other hand have a little more latitude in the way they are allowed or have been given permission to help, guide and protect you. These special Angel Emissaries are with you every step of the way, clearing your path, healing your broken heart, showing you alternatives to the issues, concerns and obstacles that you face each and every day.

Here are a few examples of how Guardian Angels help you:

- meet just the right person at exactly the right moment to help you with a project or solve a problem
- find yourself being delayed from leaving your home or office and you feel as though you may be late for an appointment; then you find out there was an accident on the street or highway you were going to use and now you have the opportunity to miss being stuck in traffic
- accidentally discover where to find the right information you need for that report, sales copy or book you are writing
- magically find something you've been searching for and were sure it was lost forever
- by comforting you when you are sad or lonely
- by guiding you away from someone; doing something or even kept away from a particular event or party, no matter how much you want to go

That has actually happened to me more than once. I have wanted to go someplace only to be re-directed or guided away from an event that I wanted to attend. In the beginning, I would try to force things to happen the way I wanted and then wonder why the results were less than desirable. Not any more, I simply allow myself to go with the flow of their energy and do something else instead. I know that there is something or someone that I don't need to experience.

While it can be frustrating to not be able to go somewhere or connect with certain people, trust that your Guardian Angels know more than you do and are protecting or shielding you from something that isn't for your highest and best good. Your Guardian Angels know you better than you know yourself. They know what you want in greater detail than you can possibly express in words or through your emotions. If you will allow yourself to be guided, you will have more harmony and less stress in your life. You will experience more synchronicity and things that appear to be coincidence than you can possible imagine!

Take a deep breath, take a step back and allow your Guardian Angels to guide you, protect and comfort you. Open your mind and your heart to these amazing Angels and watch your life, your dreams and goals start to manifest in ways you never thought possible!

How Many Guardian Angels Do You Have?

One of the questions I am asked the most is --- How Many Guardian Angels do I have? --- the answer is always the same. Everyone has at least two Guardian Angels with them all the time. At the time of our conception, two Angels accept us, to be with us our whole lives.

There are many other Angels --- like Archangels, Healing Angels and Prosperity Angels --- that can and do come and go, helping you in a variety of ways. Some people have many more Angels with them because they have "asked" Angels to come into their lives. You don't have to be "special" to have many Angels with you; however, you do have to ask.

This may upset some but here's the truth about Guardian Angels ... there are special people in our lives that have passed over .... these dear, beautiful Souls are not Angels. They are or can become Spirit Guides. My Grandfather is one of my Spirit Guides who is with me. He isn't one of the many Angels who are with me.

Sometimes someone will ask me; *How many Guardian Angels are with you, Terrie Marie*? I smile and say that there is a multitude of Angels that are always with me, guiding, healing, comforting and protecting me. Even so, I still ask for help with special projects like this one, for example. I take my responsibility of teaching as many men and women how to connect with their Angels very seriously. Some of the steps I take are grounding my energy, clearing my mind and being open to receive the information that comes through me to share with you.

What Can You Ask Your Guardian Angels to Help You With?

All you really have to do is "ask" and here's the really short version of how to do that --- Angels please help me --- that's it, straight and to the point. So, now let's give you a bit more information about how to ask your Guardian Angels to help you …

Here are a few examples of what you can ask your Guardian Angels to help you with:

#1 – You can ask your Guardian Angels to help you make the best decision for you, your work, and your Life Purpose. If you're not sure what it is that you came here to do or what your Purpose is, ask for clarity and then be open and aware of what's being given to you.

#2 – You can ask for protection on a trip, driving to work, or traveling to another state or Country. One time, a few years ago, I was traveling from El Paso to Austin, Texas, there was a lot of turbulence and people were frightened. I closed my eyes and "asked" Angels to smooth air around us. Back then I didn't even say anything to anyone about talking to Angels! Anyway, before I even finished "asking" everything calmed down including the people in the plane.

#3 – You can ask for help healing a situation, a heart-break or simply from feeling like you're all alone. In the beginning, I would close my eyes --- I can always "see" better when I close my eyes --- and "ask" my Angels to wrap their wings around me. And soon, I'd feel better. Now, it isn't the same as a hug from someone you care about BUT the feeling of unconditional love is literally out of this world!

#4 –They will help you focus on your dreams and goals, helping you become consciously aware of what you think and what you say. When you are aware of what you're feeling, thinking and saying, you can raise your inner-vibration from where it is to the next level. When you focus on what's not happening, you are focusing on the wrong end of your dreams and goals. Focus on the outcome of what you want and then become consciously aware of the signs, messages and guidance you are given.

#5 – One of the ways your Guardian Angels help you is by clearing your path mentally, emotionally and Spiritually. One of the ways this happens is to be bringing the right person or opportunity to you. It also means that people, situations or opportunities that are not a match energetically, are removed or you are simply guided away from them.

After you have "asked" for help, guidance or support, the next step is believing that you're going to get what you've asked for. If you're not getting the guidance or messages, go into meditation and be open to seeing or feeling where you can boost your own level of openness to receiving what you've asked for.

Being open, just like anything else that is new, takes practice until it becomes natural for you, trusting what you receive. The tricky part is, believing your special enough to receive the answers or help you've asked for. By the way ... you are special enough!

Getting Up Close and Personal with Your Guardian Angels

Wouldn't it be nice if you could really know your Guardian Angels are with you all the time? I mean, really feel or sense their energy around you? It is possible to know they are around you; if I can, then so can you. Before you start thinking or saying this works for others but not for you because you have to special or have special powers …. You are special and you can, if you're open enough to believe, to feel your Guardian Angels.

Here are three ways to help you get up close and personal with your Guardian Angels …

#1 – Close your eyes and take 3 deep breaths, breathe deeply and slowly and then exhale slowly and as completely as you can. Be aware of your breathing, open your mind and allow yourself to feel their loving energy around. If you can't feel it yet, keep practicing and you will.

#2 – Ask your Guardian Angels to come to you in your dreams. Have a glass of water on your bedside table and a notebook to record your impressions, thoughts, feelings or any messages you receive during your sleep time. If you wait till later you'll lose what was given to you.

#3 – Ask for a sign so you know your Guardian Angels are with you. When you ask for a sign, you can be as specific and detailed as you want. But remember this; the more details there are, the longer it will take to manifest your request. You can ask for a feather. It could be one large white feather or several smaller feathers. You can ask to see a rainbow or 3 butterflies.

These are just a few of the many ways you can get up close and personal with your Guardian Angels.

What Exactly Do Guardian Angels Do for You?

Angels are not allowed to intervene in your life unless you are in physical danger and it's not your time to transition, otherwise you must ask, it's that simple.

Guardian Angels are a part of your life whether or not you're aware of their presence. Your Guardian Angels have a bit more leeway than Angels and Archangels.

Here's what your Guardian Angels can do for you ...

#1 – They comfort you. You know how sometimes, you might feel a soft breeze against your skin but there's no air moving? I mean, the air is still, none of the leaves on any of the trees are moving, not even a tiny little bit. This is one way your Guardian Angels have of "showing you" they are with you.

#2 – They guide you away from places that aren't good for you. For example, when I first started opening back up to connecting with my own Spiritual Path and my Angels, there were times --- there still are --- when I'd walk into a shop and I would have to walk right out again. There was something, or some kind of negative energy that I wasn't supposed to be around. This is just one example of how your Guardian Angels guide you away from places or situations.

#3 – They protect you from harm. Let's say you've made a decision to go somewhere or to meet someone for coffee, and no matter what, you can't shake a feeling that you aren't supposed to go. Or no matter what you do, you're being delayed from leaving and being on time. This is a way your Guardian Angels are protecting you.

#4 – When you connect with your Guardian Angels, they will help you attract more of what you want and so much less of what you don't. The way they do this is helping you become consciously aware of what you really do want to attract and manifest into your life experience and work. As you become aware of your thoughts and how you feel, you're better able to re-focus where your energy flows, supporting your dreams and goals instead of working against yourself with self-limiting, sabotaging thoughts.

#5 – When you have questions about your Life Purpose or if you're on the right path, ask your Guardian Angels to guide you. They will also help you to know which is the right next step for you and to go about manifesting what you need to take that next step in your life or work. It's always nice to have confirmation or clarification that you're following your purpose.

#6 – They will help you heal your heart from heartbreak whether it's just happened or it is in the past. One of the ways your Guardian Angels help you heal is through forgiveness so that your heart is open and ready to love and be loved. If you have closed off your heart because you don't want to get hurt anymore, you have also closed off other parts that are essential in receiving guidance, messages and even prosperity and abundance.

    We all have questions from time to time and asking is the fastest, clearest way to get the answers you're seeking. There is no shame in asking for help to heal, for guidance or anything else in our lives. If you don't ask, it's a challenge to be able to receive what you say you want. Be open to receiving and also to giving so that you are able to receive and trust the guidance and messages your Guardian Angels have for you.

Guardian Angels Protect You from Harm

During a private session with one of my students, Margaret, who's a Jewelry Designer and Naturopathy Student in the United Kingdom, we talked about how her Guardian Angels protect her.

This is what I want to share with you now ... several ways your Guardian Angels protect you from harm ...

#1 – Have you ever walked into a shop, store, office building or a party and you immediately felt uncomfortable like something was really "off" or just wrong? That "feeling" is a warning to get you to leave as soon as possible because there is something or someone you don't need to be around.

#2 – Sometimes when I'm in my car, I get a feeling to take my foot off the accelerator. As soon as I do, another car suddenly moves right in front of me without any warning! Or maybe a car beside you in the next lane starts getting a little too close and all of a sudden that car is "moved" as if it were being pushed away from you. ... it's your Guardian Angels!

#3 - Do you sometimes get a creepy or uneasy feeling that you shouldn't go somewhere? Or maybe you've made plans to do something fun with your family or friends and at the last minute, something happens and you don't get to go. This has happened to me more than just a few times. I used to get upset; now, I just say thank you and smile knowing once again I'm being protected.

#4 – One of my students was in her car with her Fiancé at an ATM machine in the parking lot of their bank. She looked up and saw a man start walking towards them. His energy didn't feel very good or positive. She said she got scared and closed her eyes, put her fingers together, and imagined a bubble of white light around them and their car. The man started to walk in a different direction so Lauren closed her eyes again and imagined a bubble of white light around all the other cars too. The man simply turned and walked away.

These are just a few examples of how your Guardian Angels protect you from harm. There may be instances that you have been protected from harm; a car accident or being in the wrong place at the wrong time.

If you stop even for a few moments taking time to remember something that happened or didn't happen and you breathed a sigh of relief because you were protected or guided away from something or someone AND you listened and moved away. This is just one of the many ways, your Guardian Angels will let you know that they are with you, keeping you safe from harm.

How to Connect with Your Guardian Angels

There are many ways you can call on your Guardian angels to connect with them wherever you are, anytime and in any place or situation.

Here are three of my favorite ways to connect …

#1 – Writing a Letter Sharing your inner-most secrets, dreams, thoughts and feelings.

It is said, ask and you shall receive. There are so many ways to ask for guidance, signs, messages, clarification and even validation. Has anyone ever taken time to share with you just how to write a letter to Angels? Writing a letter to Angels is as easy as writing an email to a friend. Pour out your heartfelt emotions and your thoughts. Yes, Angels already know what is in your heart.

What would you write to an Angel about? What you write is your choice. I have written letters asking for healing, forgiveness, guidance, being a clear and open channel, unconditional love and acceptance.

Still not quite sure how to start or what to write? Here are a few suggestions to get you started. Use what resonates and release the rest that which does not resonate with you will guide you to what works best for you.

- Healing: Angels I ask you to heal (my friend, my nephew, my sister), please wrap them in a bubble of rose light for love, emerald green for healing at the cellular level, sky blue to soothe and heal emotions
- Forgiveness: Angels I ask you to forgive (me, my spouse, my friend) for (fill-in-the-blank)
- Guidance: Angels I ask for you guidance about (fill-in-the blank)
- Unconditional Love: Angels I ask you to help me see beyond surface appearances, seeing the Spark of Divinity within everyone to include myself
- Acceptance: Angels I ask for your help in accepting (myself, my friend, my boss, my co-worker) as they are, releasing the need to accept the need to accept abusive behavior in word or deed.
- Clarity: Angels please clear the mist, the fog from my inner sight so that I may see clearly
- Discernment: Angels I ask you to help me to know the difference between truth and that which is not truth
- Signs: Angels I ask you to give me a sign about (fill-in-the-blank)

Now it is up to you fill in the blanks, to describe in detail all you wish to share, to release to Angels.

Remember you must ask Angels to help you. Remember Angels cannot intervene in your life unless it is not your time to transition.

The key to writing your letter to your Angels is being authentic, having integrity and speaking your truth from your heart. Writing out your thoughts, your emotions or your requests infuses each and every word with your energy. It's a way of empowering, releasing, purging and detoxing your energy.

#2 – Mediation is as easy or as difficult as you choose to make it. Meditation is all about quieting your mind and calming your emotions. It's also about clearing out unnecessary Ego chitter chatter, enabling you to allow your inner guidance, your intuition or gut hunches, to become a conscious part of your mind.

Find a quiet, comfortable space where you'll be undisturbed for at least 15 minutes. Play or listen to soft music, focus your eyes on the flame of a candle, while focusing on your breathing. As your eyes are focusing on the candle flame and you're also focusing on your breathing, your mind becomes quiet.

If you take time to practice this simple meditation technique every day, you will start feeling better, raising your inner vibration, clearing your mind so you can hear the messages and guidance your Guardian Angels have for you. It's a good idea to have a notebook and be ready to write down any thoughts, sounds, or anything that seems to "float" into your thoughts. This is the start of your Guardian Angels connecting with you.

#3 - Automatic writing is a form of communication which is intuitively received or channeled through you from the Spiritual Realm and your Angels. It is receiving information or messages without editing your thoughts, without judging or filtering what comes through you.

Before you begin, it is essential to protect yourself by surrounding you and the area in which you choose to practice receiving Divine Guidance in white light. Be sure to set the intention that only Angels of the highest vibration and purest energy are allowed to connect with you. Divine Guidance is received and given in many, many forms, through a variety of channels or mechanisms. Which of these gifts resonate with you? Are you open to receiving information, messages from your Guardian Angels?

There are many more ways to create your personal 24/7 relationship with your Guardian Angels. What's been shared with you will get you started and well along your way to connecting and being aware of the messages and guidance that is waiting for you.

Everything from helping you to focus, clearing your path, healing your heart, and discovering what your Life Purpose is to being comforted and protected ... these are among the many ways Guardian Angels, your Guardian Angels help you each and every day with anything you ask them to help you with.

Guardian Angels hold your hand, clear your path and heal your heart. They are by your side day and night, waiting to be of service to you and for you. All you need to do is ask.

Chapter Two: Archangels

Archangels have a higher vibration than Guardian Angels. They are messengers of and for Divine Source. In a sense, Archangels act as intermediaries between humankind and Divine Source. These magnificent beings of Light and Love, like all Angels, are gifted with being in all places in any moment, transcending physical realm limitations of time and space as we know and understand it.

Archangels work with subtle energies to ...
... guide and assist you along your path
... answering prayers and requests for signs, messages and guidance
... open doors to limitless possibilities
... shower you with unconditional love
... infuse your body, mind and Spirit with loving healing energy
... remove energy blocks to manifesting your dreams, goals and desires

Archangelos is the Greek word for Archangel which means primary messenger or influential being of Light and Love. Inviting and welcoming Archangels into our lives, invites the gift of miracles that simply manifest in interesting and unexpected ways.

They have been gifted with the ability to transform dense, leaden earth energy through the transmutation process otherwise known as Spiritual Alchemy. Spiritual Alchemy is a Metaphysical process of removing energy blocks --- mentally and emotionally --- enabling us to raise our inner-vibration to the next level.

Archangels also protect you from harm by guiding you away from people, places and situations that are not for your highest and best good.

Archangels Guide and Assist You Along Your Path

So many men and women on their Spiritual Path, have a very deep, burning, heart-felt yearning to know what their Life-Purpose is and how to fulfill that purpose. There are many ways archangels guide and assist you along your path both seen and unseen.

Remember, you must ask Angels to help you. They are simply not allowed to interfere in your life, path or the lessons you agreed to learn for any reason --- except --- if your life is in grave danger and it's not yet your time to transition from this life back into Spirit energy.

More specifically, Archangels can help you become more consciously aware of your intuitive gifts and skills, which help you weave through fear and doubt, uncertainty and confusion about what it is you came here to do and how to do it.

When you are genuinely open to your Life-Purpose, your path unfolds before you, around you and within you as if by magic. This may sound like it's not really real or tangible but this is how it has and continues to happen in my life. I was completely clueless about what was happening in the beginning. And you know what; it still feels that way sometimes.

The best way to explain or describe this is to share a story with you … The first time I became consciously aware of Angels and their magical ways being in my life and all around me, was in 2001. I kept this very close to my heart. I had absolutely no intention of ever breathing a word of this to anyone!

We all think we want --- me included --- to know what's going to happen in the next few weeks or months. And for the most part, Angels will oblige us, giving us a glimpse of the possibilities that are in front of us in that very moment. Sometimes we even think we really and truly want to know what's going to happen down the road and/or around the corner so we can be prepared.

The truth is, if I had been privy to everything that would be required of me or that has yet to manifest, I would have said *"NO!"* shut the door and nailed it shut! Had I been given the whole, complete preview --- trials, stumbles, heartbreaks, set-backs, celebrations and triumphs --- I wouldn't be sharing this part of the journey with you now. I wanted to stay hidden and out of sight, in the shadows and most certainly in the background.

In the very beginning I wasn't even aware there were different kinds of Angels or that they all have specialties.

The first part of this amazing journey was accepting that I am different, very sensitive to energy, and teaching myself how to be comfortable in my skin --- the physical body being the vessel and channel through which Angel energy, guidance and messages would flow through me effortlessly, in time.

My path has been revealed each step of the way, one step at a time. Sometimes, these steps are easy. But in an effort to honor the commitment I made to the Angels who are guiding me even now, there have been countless Dark Nights of the Soul causing me to question everything --- beliefs, what I thought, how to trust and what faith is and even the purpose of my having incarnated.

Even when you know what your Life-purpose is, don't' expect to know exactly how each step will unfold; there are many twists along the way. If we knew what was in store for us, most of us wouldn't show up.

Archangels Answer Prayers and Requests for Signs, Guidance and Messages

There is truly no limit to the number of ways you can receive answers, guidance and messages from Archangels. The most important thing you can do is be open to receive what you've asked for. If you don't believe you're going to actually get any answers or that Angels aren't going to connect with you, you're absolutely right, you won't.

Once you've asked, trust that your request has been heard and is being honored. You can ask for a sign that is very specific, that would mean something to you and only you. For example you could ask for a certain number of butterflies, a rainbow or feather in a certain color like red. The more specific and detailed you request the sign to be, the longer it will take to manifest.

The more consciously aware you are, the easier it will be to recognize what's being given to you. The ways Archangels deliver guidance and messages are only limited to the degree that you are open to receive.

So how exactly do Archangels deliver messages, guidance and signs? Sometimes it's very obvious and at other times it's very subtle, so you really need to be observant about what's happening around you and within you. When you're talking with someone, something could be said that *pops-out* at you or really resonates.

You could be passing people in a hallway or when you're shopping and you'll hear something that makes you stop dead in your tracks or takes your breath away because you just *know* that was meant for you. You could be watching a movie or television and someone's name is said over and over again or you see something you just know is an answer to your prayers or just the right and perfect confirmation you need in that moment.

Many times when I am reading a book, it will seem as if what I'm reading is the exact answer to a question I've asked. Sometimes messages, answers, signs and guidance pop-up rather quickly. At other times it will take quite a bit longer. It all depends on what you ask and how open you are to having what you've asked for.

Guidance can come through your dreams during your sleep-time or through other people in your life like friends or family, depending of course how open they are to being a temporary channel. The reason this happens is because we want the answers or question so badly, we actually delay the arrival of the very messages and guidance we want.

Every once in a while, I'll find a feather, a white feather, inside my home in a spot that's several feet away from the garden door. Only an Angel could deliver a feather that appears well inside when the door is closed.

There are many messages that are cloaked inside number sequences or sets of repeating numbers like 111 or 245 or any combination that you see more than just two times. For example, if you see the number 444, you know there are many Angels around you in that moment. Numbers that you see over and over again are the Archangels way of getting your attention. Hearing the same song over and over on a radio is another way messages are given to you.

The key to getting answers and messages is really all about believing, trusting and being open to receive. After you have asked, take three deep breaths, exhaling as deeply and as slowly as you can. This will help you relax and open your heart and clear your thoughts.

Your questions and prayers are always answered without exception and without fail. It's up to you to set your human Ego chitter-chatter self aside to receive what you've asked for.

Archangels Open doors to Limitless Opportunities

How many times you heard ... when one door closes, a window opens? Maybe you have even said it to yourself to help ease the sting of disappointment or tried to help someone else. A long time ago I made a decision to change that phrase for myself because I wanted more than just a window of opportunity. Now I say "when one door closes, 2 new doors open, revealing new, better opportunities."

It never set well that what was being offered --- a window --- was less than I was being guided away from. Since everything --- experiences, lessons, situations and relationships --- offer gifts of healing, release and a chance to raise our inner vibration, it just resonates so much better to have at least 2 new doors open, replacing the one that closes.

There is a different word I like to use instead of door --- portal --- it is so much more expansive and all encompassing. A portal is a doorway, channel or vortex of concentrated energy.

One of the many challenges we all face on our Spiritual Journey, is not allowing ourselves to get stuck in negative energy, mentally or emotionally. Just to be clear, if we pretend or try to ignore the *rubbish* that happens, we start *stuffing* or *swallowing* our feelings. This creates blocks in the Throat Chakra and dis-ease in the physical body and ultimately lowers your inner-vibration.

Wherever your inner-vibration is, that's the exact point of attraction that is projected outward, bringing to you an exact, vibrational match.

If you're wondering what this has to do with Archangels opening doors to limitless opportunities for you, it has everything to do with it. And here's why. To be able to attract more of what you want and so much less of what you don't, your inner-vibration must be more positive, more often than it is negative. Another way to explain the importance of being aware of and knowing where you are energetically, is keeping your connection to Archangels open. When you're not at your best, it's harder to be aware of and recognize guidance, messages and signs that are being given to you.

You can ask Archangels to help you honor what you are feeling in that moment and move through it more quickly, restoring your positive mental and emotional energy to higher vibrations. It's perfectly okay to give yourself time to process what's happening and what you are feeling. Once you are able to ground, cleanse and release negative energy from your thoughts, heart center and in your environment, take a few moments to re-focus yourself.

Ask Archangels to help you re-connect with your Inner-Spirit, your dreams and your purpose. Write out what you seek to attract to you, be as specific as you can, being mindful not to create self-imposed limitations.

When one door closes, it's telling you to re-direct your thoughts, emotions, efforts and energy in another direction. This new direction, as painful or scary as it might be, is for your highest and best good, trust Archangels are with you guiding every step. Ask for help clearing your path in all ways, on all levels of vibration and in all directions of time and space.

There are so many more opportunities and possibilities in front of you than there are behind you. Trust and have faith that what's being shown to you is the next step in achieving your goals and manifesting the life you yearn to create for yourself and your family.

Take a deep breath because it gets better even if it doesn't seem like it at the time. There is always a choice to keep moving forward, stay stuck where you are or simply turn around and go backwards.

Archangels Shower You with Unconditional Love

One of the most precious gifts you could ever give or receive is *Unconditional Love*. There are many misconceptions about *Unconditional Love* and what it means or what it is. For a long time I didn't fully understand what it is, how to give and receive such a life-altering, elusive gift.

In an effort to remain authentic, in integrity and transparent, there are times and certain situations that I am not practicing or giving *Unconditional Love* to others or even to myself.

This is my understanding of what *Unconditional Love* is and how to practice giving and receiving it.

Here's what Unconditional Love is NOT; which is just as important as what it is.

*It is *NOT* about giving anyone permission to dishonor or disrespect you.

*It is *NOT* about allowing anyone to violate your values or boundaries.

*It is *NOT* about letting anyone take advantage of you in anyway, for any reason.

Now that --- hopefully --- you have a deeper understanding about what *Unconditional Love* is *NOT* ... this is what *Unconditional Love IS* all about. Taking a very deep breath, I am reaching deep within to put into words, with help from Archangels, a concept that is pure energy from Angels and Divine Source. *Unconditional Love* is the exact opposite of conditional love.

Here are a few examples of conditional love ...

*I will love you if you give me (fill in the blank)
*love or support is taken away when someone is angry or feels they have been hurt
*withholding approval or acceptance of your actions or decisions
*someone imposing their will on you for your own good regardless of what you want or need, expecting you to give and give and give without the other person giving anything in return

There are many others ways people give conditional love, but you get the idea. Conditional love is all about strings, exploiting your weaknesses, laying guilt trips and emotional blackmail to get their way. It also includes withholding affection and emotional support. Do you really want someone you had the courage to open up to secretly thinking negative thoughts about your dreams and goals or your inner-most dreams? I think not. Give what you want to receive.

You don't have to like what someone wants to do or how they live their lives. This isn't about giving anyone permission to intentionally harm someone else with words or actions.

Getting back to *Unconditional Love*, the first person to practice on is you. Can you love yourself in spite of your flaws, fears, the mistakes and missteps, the many distractions and not feeling like your living up to your own potential? Be honest. If the answer is "no" then start practicing loving yourself with all the warts, scrapes, dings, bruises and scars you carry with you in your thoughts and in your heart.

When you can love someone who has hurt you or broken your heart, you'll know you have really begun to shower others, including yourself, with *Unconditional Love*.

Now imagine having or experiencing this amazingly pure energy coming from Archangels to you, surrounding you and infusing all that you are. Angel energy is like nothing you have ever experienced. All Angels have and give you is support, total acceptance and *Unconditional Love*.

Archangels do not have conditions or judge you in any way. They just want you to know you are never alone and that you are loved beyond measure.

In those moments you fell defeated, alone, worthless or lonely, ask Archangels to wrap their loving healing energy around you. Keep asking till you feel an energy shift. You will feel a sense of calm and peacefulness within. Be open to receiving this precious and somewhat elusive gift of *Unconditional Love*.

Archangels Infuse Your Body, Mind and Spirit with Loving Healing Energy

There are times in everyone's life when they just don't feel like they can go on doing what they are doing. Something will have happened to trigger what I refer to as an Energy Wall, also known as resistance. Sometimes an Energy Wall can be so intense; it causes or triggers an even deeper Spiritual chasm, a *Dark Night of the Soul*.

A *Dark Night of the Soul* is an inner-journey questioning beliefs at the core of your Being and understanding. It is often life-changing, like a re-birthing, a complete transformation from the inside out at every level imaginable. As I write, channel and stream the information in these pages, I am being guided to share part of my personal journey with you in an effort to help you gain a much deeper understanding of what it truly means to be supported and infused with loving healing Archangel Energy.

If I haven't mentioned this before, Angels have different vibrations. Archangels vibrate higher, or faster, than Guardian Angels whose energy is more dense leave the word as it appears --- dense , which enables them to connect with you more easily.

It's no secret what I came here to do is help as many men and women with their Angels in ways that work for them and also help raise their inner-vibration so they can fulfill their purpose, with prosperity and abundance. To this end, I am often pushed beyond the limits of what I feel is possible. Each time I bump against the edge of my current comfort zone, it's time to step back, re-ground and balance once again.

Recently, I journeyed into a very intense *Dark Night of the Soul*. The last time my inner-journey plunged me into such depths had been 18 months earlier. This most recent inner-journey lasted ten days before I would begin to see even the tiniest glimmer of light. The complete cycle would last more than three weeks, from start to finish.

During this time of transition, transformation and eventual re-birth, Archangels were by my side even when I did my best to shut them out. Little by little, their loving, forgiving, compassionate, healing energy gave me hope and the courage to walk through the darkness and into the Light.

The point is, no matter whom you are, what you have done or experienced …. if you are willing to be open enough to surrender into trust and faith, Archangels will guide you through to the other side. Archangels are always with you. They only want what you want for yourself. There is no judgment. There is only compassion and a sense of harmony and peacefulness.

In those moments of complete and utter trust and faith, know you are loved beyond measure; know you have been infused with loving healing energy in the way only Archangels can fill your body, mind and Spirit. There will be a sense or feeling of deep contentment even if on the surface, things appear to have fallen apart all around you. If you will allow, Archangels will hold your hand, heal your heart and clear your path.

Archangels Remove Energy Blocks to Manifesting Your Dreams, Goals and Desires

It's all about the energy. Energy is everything and everything is energy. Before Archangels can really help you manifest your dreams or anything else, you absolutely have to raise your inner-vibration. This is true for everyone, no matter where they are on their Spiritual Path or where their prosperity and abundance levels are.

The person you are right now will not --- I repeat --- will not get you to the next level in your life and work. Now, before we go any further, this is true whether you work for someone else or have your own business or want to start living your purpose full-out. Fear and doubt cloud and cast shadows of uncertainty and is some cases, a type of *mental and emotional paralysis*. My favorite term for this kind of energetic paralysis is '*getting stuck in the muck."*

Another way of looking at *mental and emotional paralysis* is staying where you are, in your Zone of Dis-Comfort no matter how much you hurt or hate it. Being energetically paralyzed by fear and doubt, literally robs you of your hearts desires. Ask Archangels to help you dig deep, finding the inner-courage, strength and determination to take that next step no matter how frightening or difficult it feels. Don't get stuck or hung up on which Archangels to call on. It's more important to be open to asking for and being open to receiving guidance.

Focus on the obstacle or negative energy block dissolving, being blasted apart or simply melting into nothingness. Close your eyes and imagine erasing the hurt, fear and doubt. This is so simple, your Human-Self --- Ego chitter-chatter --- will tell you it simply won't work and I am telling you *airy-fairy out-there* nonsense. You will be tempted to not even try it or discount it as useless. If what you're doing isn't working as well as you want it to or not working at all, you have nothing to lose except negative energy blocks.

Write out what you want. Tell a story of what you want your life to look and feel like. Be as detailed as you want. Actually, the more specific you are, the more you channel your energy into bringing to life and manifesting your dreams, goals and desires. Archangels will help you re-focus your thoughts; eliminate old beliefs that never really worked for you to anyway.

Here's an easy way to ask Archangels to help you --- Archangels please help me with (you fill in the blank) ... help me easily recognize the guidance and messages you have for me. Thank you.

Now, this is where it gets tricky --- believe your request is heard and honored. If you're open and willing to become consciously aware of what shows up for you, you will truly be amazed. The only limit on what and how Archangels are able to guide, heal and help you, is your own imagination. Close your eyes, breathe deeply, open your heart-center and invite these amazing Archangels into your life.

You will never be the same.

Chapter Three: Angel Princes

Angel Princes are also known as Principalities or Princedoms. They are protectors, helpers and guides for mankind, representing the collective consciousness and Spirit of Humanity. Angel Princes wield a very strong and powerful influence over large numbers of people. The caveat to this is ... these Angels, just like all Angels, must be called upon or asked to intervene before their true power can be fully-invoked for the benefit of everyone involved.

One of the extraordinary characteristics of these intriguing Angels is that they attempt to guide decision makers with Universal Laws, compassion, truth, unconditional love and Divine Right Action. Angel Princes have dominion over Guardian Angels and Archangels. They are the highest ranking, energetically, in the Heaven of Form, which is the first Angelic Realm.

The Angel Princes we will explore and introduce you to are ...
... Angel Prince of the Presence Metatron
... Angel Prince of Peace Melchizedek
... Angel Prince of Light Michael
... Angel Prince of Fire Nathaniel
... Angel Prince of Death and Transition Yehudiah
... Angel Prince of the South
... Angel Prince of the East
... Angel Prince of the North
... Angel Prince of the West

Angel Princes are often portrayed as Warrior Angels wearing armor, carrying a scepter or sword. In some instances, these warrior Angels will hold a golden-white scepter in their left-hand and a gleaming, fiery white-hot sword in their right-hand. They wear a crown, symbolizing their powerful dominion over the Heaven of Form and those they are charged with guiding and protecting.

Angel Prince of the Presence Metatron

The foremost Angel of Mankind is Metatron. He is only one two Angels who were, at one time, human and were ascended and ultimately transcended from physical form into Angels of the highest-order. Metatron walked this Earthly Realm as the Egyptian Ascended Master Thoth and the Biblical Enoch. He is the original scribe, the Angelic Keeper of Records or the Book of Life.

Among the many names or titles given to Metatron throughout the Ages are: King of Angels, Chancellor of Heaven and Angel of the Covenant.

The definition of *Presence* is to be present to be mindful and consciously aware of all things at all times in all directions of time and space. The Angel of the Presence is keenly aware of all things and situations dealing with and pertaining to Humankind on all levels of vibration, in all Realms both known and unknown and seen and unseen.

Metatron maintains and manages the Akashic Records. He grants or denies access in accordance with the requestors' intentions. If your request is pure of heart, seeking insight and a deeper sense of understanding about your Life-Purpose and Soul Agreements, you will be allowed to access your Akashic Records. The Akashic Records are a collection of thoughts, events, experiences and Soul Agreements held in trust in the Astral Plane. These Spiritual Tablets are held and safeguarded in perpetuity.

The Angel Prince is a bridge between Heaven and Earth. It is said Metatron is the Angel who led the children or Israel through the wilderness and into the Promised Land.

Metatron --- He Who Walks with God --- will hear your petition to access the Book of Life, more specifically, your Akashic Records, for the sake of gaining clarity about your Soul Agreements as they relate to your Life-Purpose in the here and now.

Angel Prince of Peace Melchizedek

One of the most powerful Angels in all the Angelic realms is Melchizedek. He is known as the angel Prince of Peace, Angel of Wisdom and the Spoken Word. He works closely with Metatron for peaceful solutions for all who ask. The responsibility of instilling and maintaining peace requires great strength of presence and grace under any and all circumstances.

Presence, or to be present, is to be aware of all things in all places, in all directions of time and space and in all Realms, simultaneously. To be at peace, is to be in a state of grace with oneself, your Life-Purpose and path as your Earthly journey unfolds one step-at-a-time.

Only by becoming consciously aware of where you have been and where you are, in relation to where you are going, can you begin to tap into a higher level of awareness, experiencing a sense of peacefulness. It is about going within, an inner-journey, connecting with and tapping into Universal Source Energy. A sense of peacefulness connects us with our inner-Soul Essence. Only when we are truly at peace, can we know the true power of co-creation.

Melchizedek is charged with guiding the Nation's leaders towards peace through the teachings of Universal Laws and Truths. The natural state of our Human Spirit is peaceful bliss. When the mind and emotions are at rest, there is no conflict, fear of doubt.

In the absence of Ego chitter-chatter, there is a sense of peace within that weaves itself in and around everything we touch, say or do. The subject of peace and being at peace is a challenge because there is so much unrest all around us.

Connecting with Melchizedek and his immensely powerful energy is reassuring about what is coming through me. Now, in this moment, I am guided to be transparent about my journey of finding peace within.

The journey itself is one of surrender, surrendering chaos and confusion, fear and doubt. It is also about being consciously aware of my thoughts and emotions being stirred up by Ego chitter-chatter, causing fear and doubt, dis-harmony and losing my sense of being at peace. It is also about being willing to actively practice being peaceful, shedding anything and anyone that is not in alignment, supportive or for my highest and best good, my Divine Life-Purpose.

The Angel Prince of Peace is a calm and reassuring presence in my life. I am blessed this powerful Angel accompanies me along my path.

Ask, and Melchizedek will come into your life like a soft breeze brushing against your skin. He will help you quiet your mind and soothe your emotions so that you too can connect with your inner-Soul Essence, bringing you a sense of peacefulness into your life and experience. When you are truly at peace within, your Life-Purpose is revealed to you under grace, in magical and miraculous ways.

Angel Prince of Light Michael

The greatest of all the Warrior Angels, Michael, carries his mighty, fiery-white hot sword in the name of protection, clarity and clearing the darkness from you heart. The Angel Prince of Light is most often characterized as slaying a dragon, holding a sword and balancing the scales of justice and righteousness.

Darkness arrives as a powerful temptress disguised in many forms, including guidance from well-meaning friends and family. Words and actions can, and often do, trigger fear and doubt which appears and manifests as lack and delay, a loss of self-confidence, betrayal, disappointment and more.

Darkness surfaces, helping us face the demon or dragon on our path. When we turn to face and embrace those shadow parts of ourselves, we gain an inner-strength to take that next step into the Light of Love, Forgiveness and Freedom. Michael's sword cuts through the illusion of darkness, clearing the way for you to step more fully into the Light. Stepping out of the shadows of past programming requires courage and going within, past negative self-talk and heartbreak.

Allow Michael, the Angel Prince of Light, to be by your side, detaching negative energy attachments, neutralizing Ego chitter-chatter. In the Light, all things are revealed. The way is shown to you, distractions can be eliminated if you are willing to see the truth of fear and doubt for what it is --- illusion.

Ask Michael to wipe away thoughts of lack, fear and doubt from your mind and within your heart. There are only two emotions --- love and fear --- love is Light and fear is darkness. The Angel Prince of Light will take you by the hand and lead you into the Light.

Angel Prince of Fire Nathaniel

Fire is the most powerful element of transformation and purification. There are four elements --- Fire, Earth, Air, Water --- each plays an integral and vital part in the process of purification. The intensity of Fire energy, removes unwanted negative energy thoughts, beliefs and emotions collected and stored within the physical body.

Your Aura, the energy field that extends out from your physical body, is a mirror image of all you feel and think. During the purification process, Fire converts substance into smoke and ash. Air carries the smoke out into the Universe, dissipating negativity and magnetizing positive intentions. The remaining ashes are then given to Mother Earth and water dissolves what is left, nourishing earth. Fire is Nature's way of clearing, renewal and regeneration. The symbolic use of fire is a very quick and powerful way to cause change.

Nathaniel, Angel Prince of Fire, is also known as the Angel of Divinity, Gift of God and the Angel of Deliverance.

Call on Nathaniel to help you remove thoughts and emotions that distract you, causing fear and doubt to rise to the surface, invading everything you say and do. When there is fear, there is dis-harmony, dis-content and ultimately, dis-ease. Dis-ease causes unrest and wanting to give-up in defeat, creating a never-ending cycle of fear and doubt.

You can ask Nathaniel to help you set your intentions with the highest vibration for your highest and best good, and for the good for all involved. To burn what you have written, light a white candle. Bury the ashes in the garden or sprinkle the ashes at the base of plant.

The Angel Prince of Fire is all about assisting you in renewal and regeneration, freeing you from the past. He will lead you through the fires of a Dark Night of the Soul, helping you rise from the ashes of everything and everyone who has fallen away from you. The *burning* creates space for new growth and Spiritual expansion, preparing you for that next step along your path.

Angel Prince of Death and Transition Yehudiah

There are many Angels who are responsible for the Soul's Journey as the physical body transitions from this life back into Spirit form. Yehudiah is the Angel who chose to make his presence known for these writings.

The Angel Prince of Death and Transition, Yehudiah, is the Caretaker of Souls, accompanying all during their time of transition. Death is not always the death of the physical body. Death is about many things including, for example, transition from one set of beliefs to another more positive set of beliefs that support and empower you.

Transition arrives and shows itself as …
… the end of a relationship and the beginning of new relationships
… the beginning of a new position or career change
… stepping into the truth of who you are, stepping out of the shadows of the past
… showing up more powerfully for yourself and others, enabling you to make a difference through your Life-Purpose
… manifesting prosperity and abundance instead of lack and sacrifice

Yehudiah will guide you each step of the way to all that awaits you, all that is yours by Divine Birthright. You only have to ask. This Angel is a master of co-creating with you as you rise from the ashes of purification and transformation.

The person you are right now in this moment got you to where you are. This same person will not --- I repeat *will not* --- get you to then next level in your life or work. You will travel or journey through many transitions on your way to realizing your dreams, living your Life Purpose full-out.

The person who is channeling or streaming the information contained within these pages is not, in anyway, the same person who consciously re-connected with her own Angels in 2004. The person I am now, in this moment, will no longer exist once we finish channeling all that Yehudiah chooses to share with you through me.

The process of death and transition is an *inside job*. There is no permanent change on the outside without the necessary renewal and regeneration on the inside. Even as the Soul chooses death, there is an inner-decision or process that first begins within. Whatever the cause, intention or outcome, there must be a *Death* before *Transition* can begin.

Part Two: the Heaven of Creation

Angels of the Powers
Angels of the Virtues
Angels of the Dominions

Part Two: The Heaven of Creation
An Introduction to Powers, Virtues and Dominions

There is a natural order for every person, place and thing imaginable. Divine Order weaves in and around each one of us as our lives intertwine with each other.

The Angels of this Realm are here to help all of us with the most important relationship of all ... the relationship we have with ourselves. Relationships are simple and extremely complicated all in the same moment. Most of us are figuring things out through trial and error.

This *trial and error* is where the idea of *lessons we need to learn* came from. Have you ever heard someone say ...

... there must a lesson in all of this
... everything happens for a reason
... it wasn't meant to be
... it's a test
.. there are no mistakes or accidents

All of those statements have truth in them and yet they barely begin to accurately reflect the deeper truth. The deeper truth is what we will be exploring together as the Angels of this Sacred Realm pull back the veil, showing us how we can truly have more ...

... harmonious relationships
... peace and serenity
... transform emotional turmoil
... heal through gratitude
... surrender into trust and faith
... release all that truly no longer serves you or your purpose
... balance the gap between Heaven and Earth

We'll first journey upward and through the Powers, whose specialties are peace, harmony, balance and serenity, guiding you through emotional turmoil, creating a sense of peaceful contentment.

Next we will connect with the Virtues. These amazing Angels are here to remind humankind about the possibility of miracles, trust and faith as we free ourselves from self-limiting beliefs about who we are and what we came here to do.

The Dominions, the highest vibrating Angels of this Angelic Realm, gift us with grace along our path. These Angels are the ones who help us see past surface appearances and perceptions in the physical realm. They bring with them wisdom and mercy. They help us release the past and are the Bridge between Heaven and Earth.

Chapter Four: Angels of the Powers

This is the beginning of our upward journey into the next Angelic Realm where we get to experience the possibility that there really is a way to balance being in multiple realms mentally, emotionally, energetically and Spiritually. For years my Mom has said to me ... "Child, I don't know how you can have a foot in each realm and still function." All I could do was look at her, almost right through her as I tried to comprehend what my Mom was saying. Most of what others say actually surprises me because I am simply doing what comes naturally to me. The challenge is often putting what I see, sense and feel into words.

When I was in the 3rd grade, I was calling God, Supreme Being. No one had ever said that to me, it was just something I knew deep within. It wasn't long after my being so in-touch with Source that I flipped an energetic switch deep within, turning everything in the *off* position in an effort to be like everyone else around me.

Even when we have put our gifts in the *off* position, these Powers Angels are guarding our Soul Journey during our Earth Walk in physical form. Being in the *off* position is like being in a state of hibernation much like a bear in winter, conserving his energy, resting until it is time to once again awaken and resume our journey, living and fulfilling our purpose one step-at-a-time, and ultimately, full-out and all-in.

The Angels who are gracing us with their presence, knowledge, love and guidance are ...
... Angel of the Presence Suriel
... Angel of the Sun Galgaliel
... Angel of the Moon Ophaniel
... Angel of the Stars Kokabiel
... Angel of Peace
... Angel of Serenity Cassiel
... Angel of Harmony Trgiaob

In finding peace, harmony and serenity from within, we are much better able to tap into the flow of energy instead of offering resistance to what is, while we are creating space for what is coming through for us into our daily experience. When we are in the flow of energy, we are more aligned with the truth of who we truly are. Being in the flow, allows us to release all that no longer serves our highest and best good.

Going within, we are able to go below surface appearances, mental and emotional turmoil that prevents us from experiencing a sense of peace and contentment.

I may have mentioned this before, but just in case I haven't, there are many Angels who share the same specialties and characteristics, just like there are many who channel Angels. With that said … allow me to introduce you to …

Angel of the Presence Suriel

Suriel is an Angel of Healing. He is also known as the Angel of Death and the *Trumpeter*. As such he sounds the Trumpet of Time and Transition. Remember Death isn't always about death of the physical body, the vessel that houses our Spirit, our inner Soul-Essence during an Earth Journey. Death is also about transition, release and healing at very deep levels of conscious awareness, releasing self-limiting beliefs.

Healing occurs on many levels both seen and unseen, known and unknown. One of the most interesting things --- any maybe even a bit peculiar --- about healing is that it ripples outward from deep within our core. It's like tossing a pebble into a pond and watching the energy create the first ripple and the next larger ripple and so on.

When we allow ourselves the gift of quiet solitude, it literally creates a sense of peacefulness deep within. In part, this sense of peacefulness silences Ego chitter-chatter long enough for your entire Being to breathe a sigh of relief deep within your core.

Suriel works closely with Archangel Raphael, especially when someone has asked for healing, but their energy is too dense for Suriel to access. In other words, the higher an Angels' energy, the more of a challenge it is for us to connect. This is why Angels of the Heaven of Form --- Guardian Angels, Archangels and Angel Princes --- act as a go-between, helping us raise our inner-vibration.

Sometimes we need to heal issues that aren't even ours but we believe they are truth because we've heard it, repeated it and acted as if those issues are ours. The *first level of healing* is accepting where we are. *The second level* involves being willing to take a step back, releasing what isn't ours to carry. *The third level* is accepting we are whole, complete and perfect.

Ask Suriel to help you recognize what is yours and what really belongs to someone else. He will help you discern the truth between truth and judgment.

This powerful Angel is all about doing the deeper healing work with you one layer at-a-time, revealing the pureness of your inner-self of light and love. If you will allow it, Suriel will heal the deep felt chasm between where you are and where you want to be.

Angel of the Sun Galgaliel

The Sun is a symbol of life, light and growth, renewal, strength and courage. Energy we receive from the Sun warms the body and feeds the Soul, burning off negative energy and boosts our physical body's immune system.

Galgaliel, Angel of the Sun, helps us regulate our emotions when we allow our body to absorb the light rays from the Sun. It may sound or feel a bit weird to be reading this kind of information but this is what I'm receiving to share with you. It's also about a level of protection from the darkness that does, at times, threaten to swallow us whole, keeping us forever in the shadows and away from the light we need to thrive, and ultimately fulfilling our purpose.

One of the hardest things for most of us is to take care of ourselves first. We've been taught to give and to put everyone else first without regard for our own needs, wants and desires. If the Sun was always shining its warm rays 24/7, there would never be a completion to the cycle of rest and rejuvenation, life and death, light and dark.

Angel of the Sun, Galgaliel, helps you follow the path, your path as it is revealed to you. Being open to balance light and dark, and rest and rejuvenation is being in a state of conscious awareness about what truly works in your life and what doesn't. The power of the Sun *burns* through barriers of self-imposed limitation, creating space for self-empowerment. Part of following our path to fulfilling our purpose, is to accept our uniqueness, our strengths and our weaknesses.

In being able to accept our complete Self, we are able to experience a sense of wholeness even in the absence of what appears to be a reality filled with lack and delay. We often think if we can't see or measure growth, then it isn't happening. Significant growth is most often below the surface beyond the realm of physical sight.

The Angel of the Sun, Galgaliel, is ready and willing to light your way and your path. You can ask for healing at the cellular level, bringing all the shadow parts into the light for integration, becoming whole in body, mind and Spirit.

Angel of the Moon Ophaniel

In this Earthly Realm, the Moon dictates the rise and fall of the tides. It marks the passing of time and travels the night skies, waxing and waning, completing an ancient and timeless cycle every thirty-days. There is a sense of order within the Heavens and it is the same here in this Earthly Realm of dense physical energy. The moon is a symbol of Divine Order on all levels and in all directions of time and space as we know and understand it.

With each passing phase of the Moon, different energies give rise to different energetic intensities and emotions. They are cycles of introspection and self-reflection, growth and expansion, rest and detachment. Our life and energy flows with more grace and ease when we pay attention to the natural ebb and flow within the Cycle of Divine Order.

Ophaniel is the Angel of Divine Order, Angel of the Moon. She helps us manage the infinite cycles we experience at any given moment. Many people practice rituals and sacred ceremonies under the fullness of the Moon as it transitions into the next cycle of completion and renewal once again.

Where there is a sense of order, there is also a sense of calm. In the center of all things there is a desire for Oneness with cosmic consciousness as everything unfolds within and without. Being in the flow of Divine Order deepens our connection with our inner-self, that part of us that craves that *something more*, that deeper and higher connection with our infinite and unlimited potential. Going with the flow instead of against it, allows intuitive guidance to magically show-up in our lives and everything seems to just simply fall into place around us effortlessly.

Ophaniel is here to help us flow within the cycles of Divine Order managing emotions and energy that supports us and our purpose in all ways. When we let go, surrendering to the natural flow of the Heavens and the Universe, there is less stress and drama in our daily experience.

Ask the Angel of Moon to help you regulate and manage your internal cycles of work, rest and play. This cycle is different for each one of us and yet there is a sense of symmetry that flows within and through each of us. This flow connects us to one another as if in a cosmic dance filled with rhythm and balance … this is Divine Order.

Of course we have the gift of choice to go with the natural flow or pushing against what we know to be truth, causing resistance, lack and delay. The choice is always ours to make.

Angel of the Stars Kokabiel

Have you ever heard or said … Reach for the Stars? When I was a little girl, sometimes I would lay on the cool grass on a warm summer's night and look up at the stars and long to be among them. In my dreams at night I would fly, free to be among the Heavens, free from the confinements of my physical body, as light as a feather floating on a soft breeze. The Milky Way is like a great river of stars showing the way to infinite possibilities of unlimited abundance and access to ancient knowledge, just for the asking.

When I connect with Kokabiel, Angel of the Stars, his brilliance is magnetic. His presence gives me a feeling of unlimited potential on multiple levels of energy and understanding all in the same moment. Reaching for the Stars is all about stretching and stepping into our full potential, exceeding all expectations placed upon us by others, including ourselves.

Kokabiel is all about illumination from the inside out. What we believe can be, becomes our reality. The challenges lie in the obstacles created by lack and limitation, beliefs that become so ingrained in our conscious mind, they have become truths. These truths of self-denial are based in fear and doubt, chaos and confusion, when in truth there is only one emotion or energy that moves mountains and transports us beyond the Stars ... unconditional love.

Love is all there is. As you allow your conscious mind to expand beyond your current sense of knowing, your inner-spirit is free to soar above the struggles of lack and limitation experienced in the darkness of the physical realm. When we detach from the drama of human emotions and negative energy, we give ourselves permission to create a new reality, enabling us to flow in complete contentment along the great Milky Way.

Ask Kokabiel to help you release the gold mine within, magnetizing you to your dreams and your dreams to you. Once you have asked, be prepared for significant energy shifts within and around you. Be open to receiving guidance from this amazingly powerful Angel of the Stars, Kokabiel.

Angel of Peace

To better understand this elusive concept of Peace, the Angel of Peace asks you to close your eyes, focus breathing in and out for three full breath cycles, inhaling and exhaling as deeply as possible. As you focus on each in-breath, clear your mind, allowing all thoughts to simply dissolve and float out and away from you. As you exhale as deeply as possible, feel or sense any shadow of hurt that floats to the surface to be placed into this Angels' loving, healing hands for transmutation.

Transmutation is a Spiritual process of changing or transforming one thing into something else whether physically, emotionally or energetically. Everyone including you, has the capability of immediately transmuting negative situations, emotions and thoughts to the next higher level in as little as 60 seconds. Being able to achieve this simple, highly effective ---

not always easy --- cognitive process, can be a challenge, but the rewards create an incredibly positive ripple effect, touching and flowing through every area of your life.

Reaching deep within, we can connect with that part of our inner-self that knows and experiences only peaceful contentment for it knows only peace. Experiencing a state of peacefulness is often rather elusive as it becomes buried deep within, protecting the truth of our Soul Essence from negativity in any and all forms. During moments of lucid peacefulness, we have instantaneous access to ancient teachings and knowledge. We are able to tap into our Higher-Self, solving and resolving issues that just moments before seemed insurmountable.

The Angel of Peace prefers to remain unnamed. The intention is to become peaceful and remain as connected to the truth of who we are more often and for longer periods of time. In this way --- remaining connected and in a state of peacefulness --- we not only raise our own vibration, we also contribute to raising the vibration of this world. Allow the Angel of Peace to comfort you, and guide you through difficult and stressful situations or encounters.

Ask the Angel of Peace to take you by the hand, touching your heart-center with unconditional love and healing energy. Where there is a sense of peacefulness, there is no resistance. Where resistance ceases to exist, the flow of all you desire to have, be, do and experience simply flows to you effortlessly with grace and ease.

Angel of Serenity Cassiel

As we continue to explore the many insights among the Angelic Realms, we are given many opportunities to shed fear and doubt, transforming negative energy into positive, healing love and light. Serenity is the next higher-vibration closely following on Angelic wing-tips of peacefulness.

The Angel of Serenity, Cassiel, is associated with Saturn and depicted straddling a dragon. His sword is said to be fashioned from the mystical Phoenix, one who rises from the ashes to begin again.

Being in a state of serenity feels more like a concept rather than something that can actually be attained. While it can be elusive, it is worth practicing patience so that we can resolve conflicts, ridding ourselves of energy blocks within, creating chaos in our outer, physical world. When we are in a state of serenity on any level, we are able to tap into that part of ourselves that simply knows beyond all rational form of understanding, that our desire to fulfill our purpose is completely within our reach.

The Law of Vibration precedes the Law of Attraction on every conceivable level of mind and emotion. Where your thoughts are focused, your emotions follow. Where your emotions are focused, your thoughts follow. Being consciously aware of what is happening within and around you, gifts you with the ultimate power of choice to transform literally anything and everything you think and feel in as little time as it takes to close your eyes and complete three deep, slow, breath cycles.

It's about surrendering conflict and offering non-resistance. To be clear, surrendering is not about giving-up and giving-in. It's also not about allowing others to violate your boundaries or disrespect you in any way. Surrender is about going with the flow of energy, and allowing all that is not for your highest and best good to flow around and away from you, leaving you untouched on any level of thought or emotion. Think of serenity as a form of healing dis-ease mentally, emotionally, energetically, physically and Spiritually.

To connect with Cassiel, the Angel of Serenity, close your eyes, go within and softly *ask* this Angel to take from you all that is not a match vibrationally to fulfilling your purpose and being in a state of gratitude and appreciation at the very deepest levels possible. As you practice attaining and being in a state of blissful serenity, you will be amazed at what begins to appear into your life experience, creating a new more positive and prosperous reality.

All that we have thought, felt and experienced is a reflection in our current physical reality. To change your current reality --- no matter where you are right now --- be willing, to be willing to let go of what was as you open your mind and heart to what is coming into view for you even now.

Angel of Harmony Trgiaob

When I think about harmony and what it means, it brings images of a feather floating with grace on a barely there breeze. It is a sense of peaceful serenity taking you to the next level of calmness, trust and faith. Everything is in alignment, consciously and sub-consciously. All things --- lifestyle, purpose, thoughts, emotions and actions --- are a match, on all levels of vibration.

The Angel of Harmony, Trgiaob, helps us honor our special gifts of intuition. It's about accepting who we are, not what appears to be the truth of who we are, but, the truth of our inner-self, that of our Soul. To be in a state of harmony, is being fully and completely in the flow of energy. There is a sense of total and complete surrender in trust and full faith that you are supported in every way imaginable. It's also about knowing that as long as you are consciously aware of what is happening within you --- mentally and emotionally --- you are better able to allow the outer human issues of negativity and drama to flow around you without impacting you in anyway.

Trgiaob gently reminds us to let go of thoughts, emotions and situations that are not ours to carry. We are, of course, responsible for what is ours to heal, forgive and experience. Harmony is living in balance with the Universal Laws which govern our lives whether or not we are aware of what they are or how to work with them. It's about embracing all that we are, including our shadow-self, the parts we don't like and sometimes wish didn't exist.

The opposite of harmony is a state of dis-harmony which ultimately causes dis-ease in the physical body. I am being guided to share with you that your Aura is the first layer of protection against all unwanted, negative energy from others. The more you are able to detach from the drama around you *AND* the drama within your own thoughts and emotions, the stronger your Aura is. Stress and tension in any form, stretches the Aura out of shape, weakening and sometimes causing small tears, allowing in unwanted negative energies into you Aura energy field.

The Angel of Harmony is ready to help us be and experience harmony more often and for longer periods of time.

He also helps us release and let go of all that does not serve our highest and best good. Ask Trgiaob to help you float in a sea of complete surrender, into trust and faith. To be in harmony is to have balance in every area of our life ... work, rest and play.

As we continue to travel higher, to the next level of vibration, into the next Angelic Realm, we are asked to become more and more consciously aware of what is coming at us, and what's coming from within us. With each step along our Spiritual Path, there is more harmony and a sense of Oneness with the Angelic Realms and with us.

Chapter Five: Angels of the Virtues

Among the many gifts and blessings we are given when we invite Angels into our lives are healing, trust, faith and the freedom to choose struggle or be in the flow of effortless allowing. Choosing to surrender wholly and completely into trust and faith creates a sense of freedom that isn't easily put into words, yet this is what I agreed to do ... translating the language and energy of Angels into words as purely and clearly as possible.

As we continue taking that next step, going ever higher, expanding our conscious understanding about Angels and how we connect with each other, we create a synergistic Oneness. I strive to surrender into ever higher vibration energy streams, being an open channel to receive information Angels want us to have at our fingertips.

Recently, my time and energy have been focused in hosting a telesummit. That project, just like channeling this book, was something I was guided to do. I remember hearing myself say --- what? You want me to do what? --- Rather than resist, I took a lot of deep breaths and reached out to colleagues for help to get started with the telesummit. It's once again time to re-connect with more amazingly powerful Angels who want to share information with you about creating or allowing our dreams to manifest into physical matter.

The Angels of the Realms of Virtues are here to help us connect with our deepest heartfelt desires, practicing freedom from Ego-chitter chatter that causes distraction from our natural state of allowing and being heart-centered. Faith and trust are the keys to quieting the human-self, creating space for our dreams to flow from the Realm of Spirit into our Earthly Realm of dense, physical matter.

These Angels are here to remind us that our dreams and desires are more than wishing and hoping, they can become our reality when we choose freedom of faith and truth. Here are the Angels who have chosen to share this part of the journey with us

...

... Preceptor Angel Peliel

... Healer Extraordinaire Raphael
... Angel of Freedom Nisroc
... Angel of Trust Assariel
... Angel of Faith Uzziel
... Angel of the Written Word Asaph
... Angel of Vision Jeremiel
... Angel Pure of Heart Barbiel

While we will be exploring various facets of the manifestation process, these Angels are here to guide us on an inner-journey of healing our connection with the Divine within us. This inner healing dissolves and eliminates negative energy that creates blocks to effortless manifestation of all that is already yours in Spirit form.

Preceptor Angel Peliel

A Preceptor Angel is a teacher or primary guide, overseeing the link between Angels of the Realm of Virtues and Humankind.

My sense of this Angel, Peliel, is massive. His energy is strong, powerful and compassionate. His primary mission is to help us become mindful of our thoughts. Thoughts are the pathway to creating space to manifest what we desire into physical form. Our thoughts are the precursor to transforming dreams and desires into matter. Whatever our mind can conceive, we can achieve through trust and faith. We are not given desires only to be told "no."

The moment a thought that is fear based --- anger, hurt, betrayal, disappointment, doubt --- creeps into our mind it is essential that we stop and re-direct our thoughts to more positive ones as soon as possible. Ask Peliel to fill you with a sense of peacefulness, grounding excess negative energy. It's not about pretending that you aren't feeling what you are feeling, whatever that is for you in that moment. It is about processing thoughts and emotions that cause you to feel and be out of alignment with your truth, as quickly as possible under grace and with compassion.

Peliel is ready and waiting to help all who call upon him. No request is too small or too big. Be willing to surrender into his hands all that does not serve your highest and best good. Know you are heard. Know you will be guided and supported along your path and it will be so. All that stands in your way is Ego based fear and doubt and the need to control your every thought, emotion and action. Let go, float in total and complete surrender and all things are given to you in the moment of the asking.

Healer Extraordinaire Raphael

I've made several attempts to not use the word extraordinaire because to my human self, it feels a bit pretentious. Each time I erase the word, it is automatically re-written. So there it is... Healer Extraordinaire... as guided ... mandated by Raphael himself!

Thoughts trigger emotions. Emotions trigger a continuous loop of thoughts --- negative or positive --- thoughts that can become an endless cycle, unless you choose to stop the never-ending loop. Negative, lower vibration energy causes our Solar Plexus Chakra to become congested. I'm being given the image of a traffic jam where little to nothing is actually moving, everything is at a standstill. The Solar Plexus and Heart Chakras are intimately connected, forming an etheric energy bridge between our lower, physical Chakras and our higher, Spiritual Chakras.

Raphael, Healer Extraordinaire, is here to help us heal any and all hurt, heartbreak, pain and sorrow, in all directions of time and space, beginning with our Heart Chakra. When our heart-center is healed, filled only with love of self, love for friends and family, and love for our perceived enemies, we are free to remove the negative energy blockages in our Solar Plexus.

My understanding of the Solar Plexus doesn't follow mainstream beliefs. My belief is deeply rooted within my sense of knowing, that for me, this is truth. This may not be your truth. I ask only that you be open to what is being shared with you, then make the right and perfect decision for you.

The mainstream belief is that the Solar Plexus Chakra energy center is located just above your navel or belly button. I have always firmly felt that my Solar Plexus Chakra is located at or just behind my navel, and here's why... the moment we are conceived into physical form, we become physically attached to our biological Mother. When we are subsequently birthed out into the world as we know it, our umbilical cord is cut which then creates our navel or belly button. The Solar Plexus is the center point of our human, physical form of existence. It is also the seat of self --- self-confidence, self-empowerment and self-realization --- the point of manifestation from Spirit into the physical.

If your heart-center is only partially healed, it is more of a challenge for your human-self to clear the blocks within your Solar Plexus, creating a traffic-jam of what's waiting to be manifest into physical form. To begin the healing process, ask Raphael to come into your life. Be willing to give all your cares and worries, past pain and sorrow and heartbreak to this healing Angel for transmutation and transformation. Close your eyes and imagine his loving, healing hands on your heart-center. Feel of sense emerald green healing energy flowing into your Heart Chakra and through your entire body and out through your Crown Chakra, your fingertips and the bottom of your feet.

Healing your heart-center clears your Solar Plexus, opening your manifestation channel. Emotions, negative emotions of sadness, disappointment and hurt clog the Solar Plexus, slowing down or bringing to a complete halt, the manifesting of your heart's desires. Coming from a sense of love, dissolves negative energy congestion, opening all channels to receive your good.

Angel of Freedom Nisroc

Outdated or self-limiting beliefs cause both conscious and sub-conscious self-sabotaging thoughts, emotions and actions. Each time we stop ourselves from following guidance, we cause more lack and delay which in turn causes more fear and doubt. It is a vicious cycle of hope and disappointment in ourselves and in the outcome of our goals on our way to realizing our dreams fulfilling our purpose full-out and all-in.

We --- each and every one of us --- came here with a purpose to make a difference helping others. And yet, many of us ---sometimes this includes me --- forget to start with ourselves. In the course of my work, I meet and connect with so many amazing women and men. It saddens me that so many simply neglect themselves. They give to everyone else but don't even think about making themselves a priority in their life. The thing is, when we make time to nurture and heal ourselves first, we can actually help others in a much bigger and more expansive way than we could possibly imagine.

So, here's how freedom, the freedom to choose becomes an essential key to unlocking more of our unique brilliance to fulfilling your purpose. Simply making a decision to choose to feel and think differently shifts everything on multiple levels. I know and believe this to be truth and yet, I do find that Ego-chitter chatter will start raising objections, causing resistance. Fear and doubt are the primary emotions that cause lack and delay, keeping us in what I refer to as the "stay stuck zone" holding prosperity and abundance in all forms, just out of reach.

Being able to accept the concept of decision making as the foundation for lasting transformation as real is the first step in choosing freedom.

The Angel of Freedom, Nisroc, helps us breakthrough negative mind-sets and beliefs that stop us from moving forward, allowing us to see, think and feel differently about who we are and what we came here to do. It's about choosing self-mastery over fear and doubt caused by Ego-chitter chatter, and raising our inner-vibration. Each time we make a decision to take that next step or change our thoughts, we create space to step into more of our truth and step out of the "stay stuck zone."

Ask Nisroc to help you rise above fear and doubts, to re-focus thoughts that help you instead of hindering you. Ask for help to break-free from being like everyone else. Be willing to stand out and away from the masses of un-awakened, following your unique pathway, fulfilling your purpose and making a difference in a way only you can.

Choosing freedom is essential to transcending challenges and obstacles that cause congestion in your Solar Plexus, blocking effortless manifestation, which in turn causes more lack and delay. Believing in your natural ability to choose a new reality is as simple or as complicated as we make it. Which will you choose?

Angel of Trust Assariel

So many of us have or had trust issues. Trust seems to be one of the major reasons we humans fight ourselves and others for control. We are taught through fear not to trust strangers, places that we are unfamiliar to us and things we know nothing about. Since we come into this Earthly Realm filled with unconditional love and a sense of openness, we are deeply connected with Spirit and the Angelic Realm, despite negative mental and emotional programming to the contrary.

Coming from the Realm of Spirit into physical form to experience being human, sets-up a chain reaction that begins by absorbing beliefs --- both positive and negative --- through our DNA and becomes embedded in us at the cellular level ... that's the point of changing, healing and transforming fear and doubt into trust and faith.

Before we go any further, I want to be crystal clear ... this is not about blame or finding fault with any one. It is about becoming consciously aware of the root cause and literally choosing to dismantle the old to create a new positive, uplifting reality. To do this --- free ourselves from the past --- we must be willing to be willing to walk up to the Lion on our pathway with an open heart and open arms, facing our fears head-on with love, forgiveness and compassion.

It's another way of turning to face the shadow part of ourselves that we would rather forget and dis-own altogether. The longer we resist bringing the darkness within us into the light, we hold ourselves separate from our truth of being whole and complete.

The next step is being willing to acknowledge that we --- in human form --- are simply not in control because everyone is gifted with free will, the choice to choose to struggle or surrender. Choosing surrender does not absolve us from doing our part. It does, however, gift us with a sense of freedom to tap into the Angelic Realms to receive the guidance we crave. Surrender is giving-up negative self-talk and giving-in to a deeper sense of trusting that we are genuinely connected with the pureness of our Soul essence of unconditional love, peace and harmony.

When I was confronting the Lion of Distrust, I would imagine floating in a beautiful, crystal clear blue lake of complete and total surrender. I would close my eyes, focus on my breathing and go deep within to that place of peaceful knowing.

Assariel, the Angel of Trust, can help you let go, releasing all your cares, concerns and worries. If floating on your back in the water frightens you, ask this Angel to gently cradle your body, knowing you are safe and protected at all times. Ask for help in surrendering fear and doubt, chaos and confusion. Ask for healing at the cellular level, freeing your heart and mind from all that no longer serves your highest and best good ... and in truth, never did.

Trust evokes a sense of bliss, a deep knowing that you are eternally connected and all your material wants, needs and desires are immediately and endlessly supplied under grace in magical and miraculous ways.

Angel of Faith Uzziel

Faith and trust go hand-in-hand. From my unique perspective, you cannot possibly have faith without trust and without trust there is simply a lack of faith. Faith is knowing that, regardless of surface appearances, that everything is occurring in Divine time.

There is a misconception that there is a difference between Divine Time and Linear or Human timing. The truth is much simpler and more complex all in the same moment. The difference or gap is cause by our lack of faith that our requests are heard and honored in the moment of the asking. What gets in the way are fear and doubt and feeling we are not worthy or deserving of what we truly desire.

From the time we are very young, we are told what to believe, how to feel and how to behave so we don't bring attention or shame to ourselves and to family. This is the beginning of programming our conscious mind that can stay with us our entire lives.

But it goes even deeper than that because we inherit through blood-lines and DNA, generations of beliefs, prejudices and judgments about what is possible and what isn't. It's no wonder we humans feel there is a separation between Divine Time and Linear or Human timing. In reality we need only set Human Ego aside, close our eyes and open to the flow, allowing all to manifest into our experience.

Faith is an automatic understanding, a sense of complete and utter Oneness with Angels and the very Universe itself. It is a deep sense of perfect knowing. The conscious mind can be programmed through repetition to have "blind faith"... a type of faith that appears to defy the logic of the five physical senses.

Uzziel, Angel of Faith, is all powerful, gifting us with the ability to see beyond the present moment, connecting with the Divine Spark deep within our Heart-Center. When we connect with Uzziel, asking for his assistance in surrendering disbelief, he will wrap his violet wings around us, burning off negative energy, creating a void to be filled with Divine Love and unconditional love of self... faith.

This Angel empowers you with perfect knowing, trusting and believing that everything you seek and have asked for is already yours and manifesting into physical form. Ask for compassion in every area of your life. More specifically, ask to become empowered with positive uplifting thoughts and emotions.

The other day I traded readings with a colleague. I always "ask" my Angel Guides if I may have a reading and sometimes they say "yes". Part of the message given for me was about faith... to have the faith of a child. I've had some time to process what that means and of course, what it doesn't mean so that's where I'll start.

Here's what faith isn't... sitting back and expecting everything to be handed to you without doing anything at all. I once heard a story about a woman going to ministerial school. She was low on funds and needed food for herself and her young daughter so she started praying many times during the day and into the evening.

Then one day, the woman received a phone call that she was receiving a $500 gift certificate from a grocery store. She was so excited thinking that through prayer and meditation *ALONE*, she was able to manifest this miracle! Her daughter told her Mom that she had entered their name into the drawing at the grocery every day for 10 days. So in a way the Mom did manifest the $500 gift certificate *BUT* without her daughter physically taking action, it would not have happened.

Faith is combining trust, belief, surrender *AND* physical action. It is also about being vigilant when Ego-chitter chatter rises to the surface and begins creating doubt and fear. When we are consciously aware of what we are thinking and feeling, it's much easier to be in the flow of allowing faith to guide you every step of the way.

Angel of the Written Word Asaph

One of the most important steps to manifesting is the art of creating through the written word. Many people feel and think they can take a shortcut and simply say *the word* and it shall be so. Speaking your request silently or out loud is only the beginning. The reason it is essential to write out your intentions, goals and your dreams is because we humans tend not to fully believe in our own manifesting power through the spoken word.

The spoken word has power in the vibration it carries; yet, it often fades and disappears as soon as the next thought is formed. The absolute power of the written word infuses thoughts, emotions and energy. The physical act of writing out our thoughts requires complete focus.

Asaph, Angel of the Written Word, is quite formidable. When I was preparing to connect with this powerful Angel, his energy image came to me as vibrant Indigo, with pulsating light rays from his Heart-Center, radiating outward in all directions.

Angels of the Realm of Virtues are here to help us raise our inner-vibration to that next level in our quest for Oneness with all that we are and what we came here to do. It is much easier to just say silently to ourselves that which we desire to bring into our daily experience. When we take the time to write out our hopes and dreams and even our fears, we give voice to what we want to manifest or release with love and forgiveness.

Ask Asaph to help you create space and time to focus your thoughts and emotions into words that express your deepest desires and fears.

Whichever you choose to write about --- your deepest desires or to release fears --- always complete your writing with love and forgiveness. Then burn or tear up your heartfelt writings, releasing the energy by burning it. As you watch the writings turn to ash and smoke, trust your requests have been heard and are being honored.

The Angel of the Written Word will be by your side, reassuring you each step of the way along your path. Asaph reminds us that it is not wrong, selfish or greedy to want lavish prosperity and abundance. In the having, we are able to fully meet our needs and that of our families. In the having, we are able to live our purpose fully and completely, surrendering into trust and faith without reservation... without hesitation.

We create first with our thoughts. Thoughts become infused with emotion. Thoughts and emotions become infused with each written word. Ask Asaph to guide your writings to heal pain and sorrow and to make manifest your deepest desires in accordance with your highest and best good. Believe with your whole heart and Soul and it will begin to take concrete shape in your life experiences almost as if by magic.

Pure of Heart Barbiel

There have been moments just like this one, where I know with absolute certainty that until this very moment, I was not yet ready to channel Angel Barbiel, Pure of Heart. In ancient Eastern beliefs, the heart is the seat of the Soul. This simple, yet profound truth is something that I have known deep within before I found written confirmation. The heart also symbolizes the Soul Mind.

There is often a reference to Body, Mind and Soul as being whole and complete. If we go beyond the surface meaning, which refers to integration of the physical and that of the Spirit, we find a state of pristine consciousness. Pristine consciousness is the bridge between that of being purely human with our many flaws, and that of our Soul Essence of truth and unconditional love. It is a state of Oneness with all the heavens. As we strive to manifest our heart's desires, we must first come from that inner-space of balancing physical desire and that of and for our highest and best good.

Barbiel, Pure of Heart, an Angel of the Realm of Virtues, encourages us to purge our heart of all feelings that do not originate in truth... that of unconditional love. This Angel,

Barbiel, is here to help us heal all past pain and sorrow, disappointment and any lingering sense of betrayal however distant it is in our past. The heart is the keeper of the Sacred Texts, recording all deeds positive and negative. No matter what has or hasn't been done unto you, practice the gift of compassion and forgiveness as much for yourself as for others. No act of healing is ever complete without forgiving the Self for all mistakes... real or perceived.

Ask Barbiel to lay his hands upon your Heart-Chakra. Be willing to place all hurts, past and present, into his loving hands for transmutation, transformation and transcendence. With each asking, there is healing. With each healing there is a release. With each release, there is more peace and harmony flowing within and around you. From this state of being-ness --- peaceful harmony --- you touch that inner-consciousness of Oneness... Pure of Heart.

In the center of all things there is only love or fear. There is always a choice to love or to hate. Choose wisely. A Heart filled with fear on any level causes lack and delay in all forms of manifestation. Only that which is Pure of Heart, manifests instantaneously. In truth, there is no separation between that of Divine Time and that of Human, linear time. Imagine your entire physical body and your Aura being lovingly surrounded by Barbiel's loving, healing golden-pink energy.

It is time we all become more aware of those jewel-like moments of absolute peace and harmony. In those moments, we are tapped into our truth of love and light, manifesting our truest desires for happiness, success, love, wealth, health and prosperity and abundance.

In the absence of fear, all is made manifest, in support of that which you came here to do... make a difference in the world, by first raising your inner-vibration through the prospering power of love.

During the channeling of this chapter, my own journey would take me through two separate, very distinct Dark Nights of the Soul, purging my Heart-Center of a core issue I believed to have been completely healed. Without going into details, it is that sense of abandonment on all levels, not just those in this Earthly Realm, but also from the Angelic Realm. There are times, still, I feel alone and out of place longing to be elsewhere.

Then ever so gently, all things begin to once again fall into place on yet a higher-level than before... and the cycle begins again.

The cycle is one of integration and assimilation, healing, Spiritual Expansion, sharing messages and guidance, stepping into the light more fully, living my purpose full-out and all-in, benefiting everyone. The next part of this journey takes us even higher, rising above all that has come before, bringing us to where we are now, this moment.

Chapter Six: Angels of the Dominions

In recent years, I have discovered a truth so profound, it will impact life as you know it ... it did mine. This being my first and only incarnation into human form, I have struggled for most of this lifetime to understand and de-tangle the many intricate levels of energy, especially those energies of pain and sorrow in all forms.

I studied for a short time with a mentor to master my own money-mindset. In his teachings he states that we inherit beliefs through our DNA, passed down from generation-to-generation. This one simple, powerful concept helped me unravel the mystery of Karma and the necessity of healing issues I just *knew* were not mine, causing a life-time of unnecessary struggle and heart-ache.

Most of what we carry in our hearts and minds --- the emotional and mental baggage --- isn't even ours. The past has become part of our present because we haven't yet begun to truly untangle truth from judgment and illusion.

When we heal --- truly heal at the cellular level --- we are gifted with forever changing our energetic vibration. And it doesn't stop there. As we raise our inner-vibration through love, mercy, compassion, kindness and empathy, we are literally sending and receiving healing both backwards through previous generations and forward, into the present moment and beyond.

Make no mistake, the human condition I refer to as Ego-chitter chatter will attempt to distract you with long-forgotten emotional triggers that could send your Spiritual-Self seeking shelter from the impending negative energy storm ... sometimes referred to as a Dark Night of the Soul.

Angels of the Realm of Dominions are here to help us navigate and manage the Dark Nights of the Soul through forgiveness, reconciliation and grace. These empathic Angels are the bridge between the Realm of Spirit and this Earthly Realm of dense energy and substance. Being able to bridge the realm of the unseen and intangible, is essential in our continuing quest for that elusive sense of Oneness. In truth, we are always One with Divine Source.

The Angels of Mercy, Grace and Compassion who are accompanying us for this segment of our journey are ...
... Angel Chief of the Dominions Hashmal
... Angel of Scent, God's Sweet Perfume Muriel
... Angel of Divine Justice and Balance Zadkiel
... Angel of Remembrance Yahriel
... Angel of Reconciliation Meher
... Angel of Mercy Ra'amiel
... Angel of Forgiveness Balthiel

The Realm of Dominions oversee that which is now behind us, retaining lessons learned through the gift of remembrance, enabling us to lay-down inherited negative energy beliefs and burdens of the past. It is important to remind ourselves there is no room for blame or judgment. It's not about casting our perceived burden on to others. It is about laying all to rest with unconditional love, forgiveness, compassion and mercy.

In forgiveness and through compassion, we transform pain and sorrow, freeing our inner-Spirit, our Soul Essence from shadow and darkness, encouraging us to step into the light in a state of grace.

Angel Chief of the Dominions Hashmal

As I close my eyes to connect and see what will come through me for you, I hear the word or name Hay'yah. The energy of this Angel feels violet, deep bright blue-violet, edged in radiant gold. I have in my left hand two crystal wands to help me focus in on this energy. As with each Angel, it is different from all the others. I am being told, Hashmal, who is the Chief of the Angels of the Realm of Dominions, is adamant that his messages of hope, compassion and mercy through states of grace are told. His benevolent nature is quite unyielding in managing this Angelic Realm.

Forgiveness of Self is the way of this Realm, where compassion is the channel through which all sins --- real or perceived --- are transmuted through the power of fire energy. Violet is the highest-vibration of light and color humans are able to visibly perceive.

Hashmal is known as the fire-eating Angel. The image I'm being given is one of this compassionate Angel closing his all-seeing eyes, arms outstretched to receive all thoughts and emotions that no longer server our highest and best good. His powerful lungs fill with all petitions or prayers for healing and forgiveness. As Hashmal of the Hay'yah (Dominions) inhales deeply, all is consumed in the Great Flames of Grace within his belly. As he exhales, all petitions have turned to soft white-violet light breaking-up all that has been carried in both heart and mind for generations. This Angel's sole purpose is hearing the countless petitions and prayers brought to him through the multitude of Angels who are in service in this Angelic Realm, to Humankind.

My body temperature is rising as Hashmal channels his messages of hope and renewal through me for you. This is just one way Angels gift me with confirmation and validation that what is being written is truth. We never burden Angels with our requests for healing and forgiveness. It is through forgiveness that we are able to balance all that has been given to us and all we pick-up along the way.

Ask Hashmal of the Hay'yah to help you use your gift of discernment to know which beliefs are rooted in truth and those born of illusion. Once you have taken the time and identified that which is truth and that which is illusion, it is time to let go of all illusions. No matter what you are facing in your life, Angels are always with you, to comfort, heal, protect, love and guide your footsteps. It isn't always easy to simply let go and let God and Angels help us. Many times we have allowed ourselves to identify with past experiences, especially the negative ones.

Hashmal helps us create a new, more positive and empowering identity, freeing us to discover and live our purpose with grace and ease. The more we are able to detach from the past, the more we are open to live more fully in the moment and raise our inner-vibration. Living in the present moment enables us to reconcile the past. If we are stuck in the past, we cannot possibly move forward manifesting our deepest desires.

One last thought before leaving Hashmal, we aren't given a desire only to have it denied us.

Angel of Scent, God's Sweet Perfume Muriel

I truly love the way Angels have of expressing their presence through me. I always "ask" each Angel what he or she wants me to channel on their behalf. This moment is no different. I am sitting in one of the my favorite coffee shops with a pile of Angel books, my crystal wands in my left hand, crystal bracelets on my wrists and crystal pendants round my neck and a smile on my face.

Muriel, the Angel of Scent, tells me oh so softly that there is an odor to darkness and shadow. I smile because this makes absolute and perfect sense even though this is the first time I have heard this truth. When you think about it for even a moment, flowers and trees that are healthy and blooming, have a wonderful scent. The plants that are not doing well have the smell of rot and decay... that of death and dying.

Have you ever walked into a shop or room and all of a sudden found you couldn't breathe or your head started to hurt? I have and I turned right around and walked out. Scent is pleasant. Odor is foul. Love is light and sweet. Anger is heavy and sour.

All thoughts and emotions are energy vibrating at different levels of light or darkness. So now we are given another way to rise above fear and doubt, anger, pain and sorrow. The longer we hold onto anything that caused us pain or heartbreak, the more we taint our energetic scent. Darkness seeks its match. Light seeks its equal. Both frequencies seek to manifest more of the same.

Here are a few ways you change your energetic scent and point of attraction...
... meditate for at least 15 to 20 minutes
... detox your physical body by taking a salt bath
... detox your environment with incense
... call-in Angels to help you transmute negative thoughts and emotions

To connect with Muriel to raise your inner-vibration, she asks you to close your eyes and imagine your favorite flower and inhale the scent through your nose as deeply as you possibly can. As you exhale, imagine the negative energy leaving your body. Repeat this process until you see or sense your breath to be a beautiful shade of golden-yellow. A word of caution... you may see or sense a different color... that is perfect. Go with that. Everyone is different and unique. Maybe you are someone who has the gift of scent like some of my clients. Sometimes I do pick-up a scent of roses or a sweet smelling aroma of myrrh when the air is still.

Ask Muriel to help you raise your inner vibration through the power of scent and aroma. The happier your thoughts, the better you feel. And the better you feel, the higher your energy, the deeper the healing. Remember to also ask for compassion during this heightened sense of healing.

Ego-chitter chatter will do its best to distract and even attempt to pull you backwards because this is just too simple to work. It isn't easy but it doesn't have to be difficult either.
As we continue to climb higher and higher, what we think we know will be challenged. Be mindful of the thoughts and emotions that will be triggered as you wave your way past generations of negative beliefs and self-fulfilling prophecies of lack and limitation.

The Angel of Scent, Muriel, is an Angel filled with grace, compassion and unconditional love, allowing her to intercede on our behalf. Through love and forgiveness of self, all channels are clear and all doors are open to receive your endless good, under grace.

Angel of Divine Justice and Balance Zadkiel

All things must balance, that is Law. It is the Universal Law of Giving and Receiving in its purest form. Here's what I'm being given ... in all things there must be balance. If we are in a state of anger, we project and radiate dense, dark energy with a foul odor. Conversely, when we are in a state of happiness, no matter the reason we project and radiate soft, light energy with an alluring and inviting scent.

Negative energy repels prosperity and abundance. Positive energy repels lack and delay. It is that simple and that complicated. There are far too many instances of injustice... one person doing or saying something to another for selfish gain without regard to the outcome. At some point, *ALL* karmic debts are settled. This is Law. The sooner we are able to truly forgive the transgression and the transgressor, the sooner we free ourselves to begin manifesting and receiving our endless good.

Many years ago when I was still living in Hawai'i, I was painting tropical flowers and colorful reef fish on canvas tote bags and watercolor paintings. I was so excited to have received a big wholesale order! The shop owner knew the pricing and was well aware of what he was ordering. When he received a copy of the purchase order; he quickly back-pedaled and offered to accept the complete order on consignment. Back then I wasn't connected to Angels the way I am now but I knew there was something very wrong. We negotiated the order to a fraction of the original order with payment in full, due in 30 days.

Can you get a sense of where this is going? You are spot on... 90 days came and went without payment. I went to the shop in Waikiki to collect my payment. Skipping ahead a bit, I reclaimed all unsold inventory. It would be another two weeks before I received payment for what had been sold. Within 60 days, that shop closed its doors for good.

It wasn't what I wanted. What I wanted was to have a fabulous outlet in Waikiki and work with amazing shop owners. Even then, I was protected from what could have been a rather devastating experience. And the Universe balanced the books on behalf of everyone who had been cheated.

If there is something that has happened to you, or someone you know and love, ask Zadkiel for Divine Right Action, Justice and Balance in all things. You may not ask for a specific outcome. That would be imposing your will and you'd be attracting back to you what you're projecting out into the Universe.

The Angel of Divine Justice and balance will act on your behalf, you need only ask.

Here is an example of how to ask for a specific outcome without incurring karmic debt ... *Zadkiel I ask for Divine Right Action, Justice and Balance. I want to see my kids, I want a reasonable amount of child support to be awarded to my soon-to-be ex-wife/husband. I want and need to be able to support myself and I want to see my kids every week. Thank you.*

You get the idea. I use that example because it is all too common during a divorce that one spouse attempts to take the other for everything they possibly can, regardless of what's right and reasonable. No matter what, no matter how long, the Universal Law of Giving and Receiving will be balanced through Divine Justice or retribution. In Hawai'i we are mindful of boche (ba-chee)... what you wish upon someone will come back to you tenfold.

Be careful what you wish upon others, it will come back to you in one form or another .... It always does!

Angel of Remembrance Yahriel

There is a fine balance between remembering the past and facing the future through the present moment reality. Buried in that which s now behind us, are memories happy and sad, positive and negative. There are dreams and goals both realized and those that remain unfulfilled. The balance is between retaining lessons learned and releasing pain and sorrow through forgiveness healing.

It's also about remembering we are always connected with and surrounded by Angels. Within an inner-knowing that we are one with Divine Source, is a sense of peacefulness in which anything is truly possible. The purpose of remembering is not so much about keeping you "in your place" as it is meant to be a Spiritual roadmap, a guide around, through and into the light.

Yahriel, Angel of Remembrance, is ready to take you by the hand, leading you through the shadowy depths of all that is now behind you. As memories rise to the surface of your conscious mind, we are given a choice as to how they will or will not affect our present reality.

The act or gift of remembering is an opportunity to...
... re-learn
... re-visit
... pass through
... forgive and release
... creating space for what we truly desire to manifest into concrete experiences in our life.

Ask Yahriel to help you discern the difference between the past rising to the surface as a guidepost or that which needs to be release through healing. The Angel of Remembrance will help you lay to rest all that no longer serves you and your highest good. Clearing out past memories through forgiveness, unconditional love and compassion is the key to seeing past surface appearances of lack and delay. The more we are willing to see truth as it is present to us in our current reality, the easier it is to reconcile the past.

Angel of Reconciliation Meher

Reconciliation is the conscious act of integrating two or more facets of ourselves together into Oneness. In truth, we are One with our past, present and future experiences and opportunities. In the absence of carrying forth the burdens of the past, we are gifted with the freedom to no longer carry false beliefs in our thoughts and heart-center. With each release, we move forward into the truth of who we are, more fully and completely. There is only light. There is only love. Fear is but an illusion to keep us small and in the shadows of emotional and mental bondage.

To move forward towards living our purpose and raising our inner vibration, we must accept the wholeness of who we truly are ... light and shadow. The shadow is that part of our truth we would rather forget, even to the point of denying the darkest parts of our human existence.

As I *seek to connect* with Meher, I *see* a brilliant Angel bathed in soft golden robes, holding a lantern high above his head. The image I'm given to share with you is filled with light radiating outward and penetrating all layers and levels of time and space.

If we feel separated from our Divinity, how can we expect to feel or believe we are whole and complete? Bringing our shadows into our present, does not mean we are opening ourselves to something or someone negative. It does mean, we are willing to accept all that we are. The truth is, all that we are, brought us to where we are now. To get to where we crave to be, we must choose to reconcile the past into our present.

Ask Meher, the Angel of Reconciliation, to help you heal all that attempts to keep you distracted by past pain and sorrow. Ask for help recognizing the difference between what is yours and that which is not yours to carry. Be willing to let go of the beliefs you have carried within your heart-center as your own ... lay them down with love and simply let go.

In the Light there is justice and mercy. Be compassionate with yourself as your inner-journey guides you from the shadows of what once was, and into the light of what is and what will be.

Angel of Mercy Ra'amiel

My understanding of mercy is that it encompasses kindness, compassion, understanding another's point of view, love and empathy ... all of which are a part of the whole. To show mercy to others, we must first give ourselves permission to see past our perceived shortcomings in character and belief in our being worthy of manifesting our dream of living our purpose.

Empathy is the ability to understand what someone else is experiencing without having to fully immerse ourselves in the situation at hand. If you are an empath --- someone who is extremely sensitive to energy --- being compassionate gifts you with intuitive insights into how to be merciful.

Because of past programming, we assume the task of judging and possibly condemning ourselves. Even after we are no longer in the presence of those who have belittled us and caused us to devalue our truth, we attract to us similar situations and relationships. Being merciful is nurturing yourself through the many layers of acceptance, release and ultimately forgiving you for any mistakes you feel you made along the way.

Ra'amiel, Angel of Mercy, shows us how to be merciful first to ourselves and then to others. It is very easy to judge and condemn each other and ourselves. We have tongues that cut using words designed to hurt, sometimes beyond repair. Words can be given to uplift instead of tearing down. Ask Ra'amiel to help you hold harsh words before they leave your lips. Words, kind or harsh, once spoken cannot be undone.

We have the power within us to forgive through mercy, kindness and compassion ... all are expressions of unconditional love. Ask the Angel of Mercy to guide you through anger, hurt and disappointment and into the light of unconditional love and mercy.

Ra'amiel's green-gold energy heals and seals the past, leaving all that no longer serves you, behind you where it belongs.

Angel of Forgiveness Balthiel

Forgiveness is such an important and essential part of the manifestation process and here's why … when there is any thought or emotion that lowers our inner-vibration, there is something to forgive. In its most simplistic form, forgiveness is releasing you from an emotional prison. Any negative emotion causes lack and delay to attracting prosperity and abundance, clients and customers and being able to recognize and say "yes" to opportunities instead of hiding out in fear of not having enough.

Being able to truly forgive others and ourselves in the process, not only clears all channels for increased giving and receiving, it also raises our inner-wealth frequency. It isn't about saying that what someone said or did was okay or that you are opening yourself up to attracting more of the same. It is however, giving you permission to let go of the hurt, freeing you to move forward. Anytime we are able to let go of anything --- and anyone --- that feels like a burden, we raise our inner-vibration.

The Angel of Forgiveness, Balthiel, will help you understand the truth of forgiving others and yourself. He will help you go below the surface of the pain you feel so you can get to the root cause and release all that no longer serves you. Ask Balthiel to help you detach from the drama, so you can *truly see* how to free yourself with love and compassion. He helps you surrender and accept the past as part of who you are and embrace the present with an open heart.

Ask for help with emotional healing, releasing you and your heart from painful memories and experiences. You can ask for guidance to create healthy boundaries to empower you. Be willing to accept responsibility for your actions, the part or parts that are yours. This isn't about assuming full and complete responsibility for everything. This isn't an easy part of your inner-journey. It is essential if you are going to move forward, being open to receive all you want, need and desire.

Thoughts and emotions that lower your vibration, also lowers your point of attraction. When your point of attraction is low, you attract less of what you want and more of what you don't want ... that is the Law of Vibration. Don't believe me? Look around at the experiences and people in your life. Are you able to connect with your Angelic Guides? Are you getting the guidance, messages or clarity you want? If you answered no to any of these questions, you really need to raise your inner-vibration.

Our journey through the Heaven of Creation and the Angelic Realm of Powers, Virtues and Dominions is now complete. Each Realm has its specific purpose in helping us heal our relationship with ourselves and with the people in our lives, past and present.

On every level, there is healing work to do. I do wish there was a point of completion. Unfortunately, healing continues as we keep on reaching for that next level of Spiritual Expansion, increased prosperity and step out beyond our comfort zone into the unknown in trust and faith.

As you open yourself to all that is shown to you, you will begin to sense energy shifts more intensely and more frequently. This is nothing to be alarmed about, just remember to breathe and ask Angels to help you embrace these changes with an open heart.

Next we journey upward still, into the Heaven of Paradise exploring and connecting with Angel's whose vibrations are extremely high.

Part Three: the Heaven of Paradise
Angels of the Thrones
Angels of the Cherubim
Angels of the Seraphim

Part Three: The Heaven of Paradise
An Introduction to Thrones, Cherubim and Seraphim

The very word Paradise conjures visions of a state of being where there is only love and a sense of Oneness on all levels that is pure joy and bliss. In this place, there is no feeling or belief in separation because Ego simple ceases to exist as we know it. To gain entrance, we are asked to raise our consciousness, open our hearts and empty our minds to experience the Angelic Messengers of this Realm and of the Divine.

The Angels of this Realm are here to help us step beyond everything we have ever known, believed and trusted to be truth. We will be asked again and again to shed the Human conditions of denial and separation. This is the Realm in which we are encouraged to surrender all illusion, enabling us to experience complete and utter Oneness with Divine Source.

The Heaven of Paradise opens its Ethereal Gates, gifting us with unconditional love, wisdom and the ability to experience effortless co-creation in its purest form. Here, our Soul is attuned to Divine Wisdom. There is no separation between our will and that of the Divine. Everything is expressed through Oneness Consciousness.

We continue to journey ever upward into the highest Angelic Energies known to Humankind. As we continue to ascend, the energetic vibrations are lighter and have an intensity that requires our intentions to be Heart-centered without Ego attachment.

We'll first journey through the Realm of Thrones. Angels in this Realm are pure thought, transforming thought into matter in this Earthly Plane. The Thrones guide Humankind with being the moment, fully and completely present to experience the countless blessings in our lives.

Next, we will journey into the Cherubim who are all-seeing and all-knowing. When we are centered, open to receiving wisdom and knowledge, it is Angels of this Realm who assist us in knowing all is in Divine Order, unfolding perfectly.

Finally, we come to the Seraphim, the highest and most divinely radiant of all Angels. Angels of this Realm are Celestial

Beings of Bright White Light. They represent the very Essence of Creation itself.

Chapter Seven: Angels of the Thrones

Once again we begin this journey into another Angelic Realm whose vibration is higher than the one before it. The Prophet Ezekiel saw the Angels of the Realm of Thrones as wheels of fire with many eyes. These Angels of Justice exist beyond form as we understand it. They are sentient Beings who assume form as swirling streams of rainbow light.

Angels, who reside in this Realm of Thrones, are reflections of faith, power and the Glory of the Creator. These Angels offer us solace as we weave our way through thoughts and emotions in an effort to manifest our dreams, wants, needs and desires.

When we are fully present in the moment, we are fully focused on all levels of consciousness. Being fully present opens all channels and pathways for full and complete manifestation. Thrones Angels helps us transform pure thought into physical matter. Here in their presence we are gifted with the ability to suspend identification with human Ego.

The Angels who are present, drawing us ever closer to a state of pure, heart-felt co-creation are...
... Angel of Unconditional Love Jophiel
... Angel of the Sacred Inner-Self Orifiel
... Angel of Truth and Clarity Ambriel
... Angel of Being
... Angel of Power and Glory Sandalphon

We are able, if we so choose, to enlist the help of Thrones as co-creators. To create a new more powerful reality, we must dismantle our current reality which is based primarily on illusion. As we step out over the edge or everything we have ever known, believed and trusted, we are literally surrendering into nothingness ... a deeper sense of Oneness with our true nature of light and unconditional love.

Angel of Unconditional Love Jophiel

The first time I heard the words *unconditional love*, there was no frame of reference to help me understand what this meant or could mean. The concept that anything, much less love, could be given without conditions of any kind was completely foreign to me.

How was it possible to love in this way? As I read books about Soul Love and how to forgive, I began to realize *unconditional love* was the exact opposite of what I was given as a child and into early adulthood. One day I realized it was the exact opposite of everything I had *ever* experienced.

Knowing the difference between conditional and unconditional love is just the beginning. The sense of openness and that of pure love, is what we --- all of us regardless of present circumstances --- brought with us from the Realm of Spirit as we transitioned or transformed into physical form.

The Angel of Unconditional Love, Jophiel, is here to guide and counsel us without conditions of any kind regardless of our previous experiences. Ask Jophiel to help you open your heart like a rose whose only purpose is to share and express beauty with the unfolding of each petal. As with all things, coming from the heart without conditions, without judgment requires practice, diligence, patience and conscious awareness.

Imagine you are in a garden with thousands upon thousands of Roses of all colors and sizes. Close your eyes and while the scent of these colorful symbols of love fills the air ... feel the vibration of love fill your senses and your body. Jophiel will take you by the hand, guiding your every step around the countless unnamed self-worth obstacles. As you begin to truly love others, you will be able to give unconditional love regardless of circumstances.

Ask the Angel of Unconditional Love to clear your thoughts, your energy and your heart of everything and fill you with a sense of peace and harmony. Breathe in rose or deep pink light. See, feel or sense the energy of love fill your entire being. Jophiel is with you, wrapping her wings of unconditional love around you.

Admittedly, even after more than 20 years of practicing giving unconditional love, unconditionally, I catch myself having conditional thoughts and feelings from time-to-time. In an effort to be completely transparent ... when someone hurts me or sends negative thoughts and energy my way, it can be an effort to project unconditional love.

The more you are aware of what you think and feel, the more often you will experience unconditional love for you and the people around you. It's all about being willing to go within, to the very center of who you are ... pure light and unconditional love.

Angel of the Sacred Inner-Self Orifiel

The Sacred Inner-Self is also known as the Divine Flame within or the Spark of Divinity. It is in this *inner-intuitive-sanctum* that our Soul Essence, the utter and complete truth of who we are, connects us with the Universe and a profound a sense Oneness with Angels and Source itself. Within the sacredness of our Inner-Self, we're able to float in total surrender, trusting that all our needs, wants and desires are met, exceeding all expectations imaginable. This is where we are asked to open our minds and hearts, accepting as truth all that is shared with us.

We often speak about connecting with or tapping into our inner-intuitive guidance only to discount or de-value ourselves and what we receive in the process. The degree, with which we are open to receive and trust, is the degree of depth of our ability to receive all we have asked for and claim as part of our Divine Birthright.

Orifiel is our guide to connecting more fully and completely with our seemingly, elusive Sacred Inner-Self and our innate intuitive gifts, unlocking our Divine Birthright of being fully present, co-creating our truth into physical matter ... manifesting our heart's desires. His robes are golden-read, trimmed in Emeralds, Rubies and Sapphires. Orifiel radiates a sense of sacredness into our open hearts.

Everyone I have ever spoken with, whether they are on their Spiritual Path or not, crave that feeling of being whole and complete. The Angel of the Sacred Inner-Self, Orifiel, will help you go deep within to touch your Soul Essence, re-igniting the Flame of Divinity within.

Ask Orifiel to help you step out of your comfort zone of fear and doubt, laced with lack, delay and disbelief. Ask for the roadmap into your Inner-Self and prepare yourself for what begins to transform from Spirit into definite concrete shape in your Earthly experience.

Only when we are truly willing to leave everything behind us --- fear and doubts, chaos and confusion, feelings of betrayal and abandonment --- can we fully embrace the unparalleled magic of co-creation.

Angel of Truth and Clarity Ambriel

We begin with a brief interpretation of truth ... what it is and what it isn't. A truth is that which is Universal, an expression of a state of being or concept that transcends the perceptions of Humankind ... truth stands the test of time, language and the appearance of human reality. It isn't something, a concept or statement that has been said and repeated, countless times, becoming an accepted belief. A belief, over time, becomes a truth simply in the ceaseless telling of a single story. This form of truth is, simply stated, an illusion.

When I think about what the word clarity truly is, a line from a song comes to mind --- I can see clearly know the rain has gone --- my shoulders relax and all I have been *carrying* seems to melt away. Another way to express the concept of clarity is the absence of every thought and emotion that creates a sense of separation from our inner-truth of being whole, complete and perfect just as we are right now in this moment. It is a gift of being able to see through the illusion of fear and doubt and into the light of love for self.

So many of us have --- maybe to a certain extent you still feel this way --- felt like the walking wounded. There was a time I felt like I was completely alone even when I was in a crowded room. Truth be told, sometimes I still do. That's how much of an effect my early-childhood programming had on me. There are moments, even know, when everything I *know* to be truth is questioned, shaking me to my very core.

With each forward movement towards our desire to make a difference fulfilling our purpose, we become mindful of the difference between truth and illusion. As each Universal Truth reveals itself, we peel back the veil between the Realm of Spirit and our Earthly existence, giving us the gift of seeing clearly.

Recognizing truth and having clarity are forms of communication at the highest levels of vibration accessible to humankind. When we give ourselves over to trust, faith and unconditional love, we are able to fully grasp the meaning of being crystal clear about who we are and what we came here to do ... and the truth that sets us free.

Ambriel, the Angel of Truth and Clarity, awaits your request for guidance through the labyrinth of darkness and illusion, the programming which caused each of us to doubt everything and everyone through the lens of fear and suspicion. He will take you into his arms protecting you from negative energy and its harmful effects with his mighty wings of Red and Silver.

Ask Ambriel to take you by the hand, leading you through the maze of untruths and blurred vision, to truth of purpose and clarity of vision. This Angels is eager to reveal to you, the truth of who you are, giving you the gift of knowing the next steps to take along your journey with courage, empowering you to new heights.

Ask to have the layers of self-doubt erased and replaced with a sense of knowing that fills every fiber of your *Being*. In those moments of self-doubt, stop and breathe tapping into this sense of utter and complete surrender into trust and faith.

As you re-connect with your truth, you will once again have access to clarity of purpose. Ambriel is always by your side, guiding your every breath, thought and footstep. Be willing to let go of all that no longer serve you and your highest-good.

Angel of Being

To *BE* is to exist as both energy and as a physical vessel, which is the keeper of our Soul Essence of Light, Love and Truth. A State of Being is a blend of our conscious and sub-conscious minds. In this *energetic space where the two minds intersect*, we are able to experience a sense of total and complete Oneness.

In that somewhat elusive State of Oneness, there is a *sense of nothingness*. This *nothingness* is not lack in any form, thought or emotion. It is simply and completely all-encompassing, a blend of light and dark and all things in between. In this space we know all, see all and are all. We are pure energy … pure thought, capable of conjuring or manifesting immediate and endless supply.

In truth this omnipotent gift is within and around us to honor our every request. We have chosen to set aside this truth through the ages in an attempt to control our very existence, manipulating Universal Law to benefit only the most powerful among us.

The Angel of Being chooses to remain nameless because the intention is for you to associate and connect with that part of your existence that is pure energy, light and unconditional love, transcending identification with human ego.

The Angel of Being asks each of us to let go and abandon the desire to dominate and control every aspect of life as we know it. We are encouraged to consciously manage our thoughts, emotions and our actions, surrendering that which does not and never has served our Higher-Self and that of our Divine Purpose.

This Angel's energy is omnipotent and omnipresent. The Angel of Being can only be accessed through meditation and in a state of balance and peaceful harmony. He is all powerful and benevolent, extending his hand to us, guiding our minds and hearts to that inner sanctuary of our Soul Essence and that of our Soul Purpose.

This part of our journey requires us to be mindful that we not only seek to heal our own inner shadow-self, we also seek to heal the planet through love, the highest of all vibration and that of Divine Source. I am blessed to be able, at times, to experience a sense of tranquility that is truly beyond expressing in words. It is a space in which there are truly no limits, only a sense of wonder at the peacefulness on all levels of knowing. Even so, I asked how to share this experience so others are able to identify their experience of *Being*.

Many, many years ago while my family still lived in Hawai'i and I was in school here on the mainland, I experienced for the first time this sense of utter calm and peacefulness. I was going to school in Columbia, Missouri. In the winter-time I wore 2 pairs of socks to keep my feet warm. One morning I woke to find what I can only describe as a winter-wonderland! As I walked outside, there was a quiet so profound it filled me with a stillness unlike anything I had known before. The trees were wrapped in ice, creating a kaleidoscope of rainbows dancing on the thick blanket of white covering the ground.

I remember standing completely still; nothing else existed except this slowing of time. I turned slowly to take in as much of this amazing scene as possible. To this day, I need only close my eyes to re-connect with that experience. It felt like I was in a snow globe. Everything was still ... no people, no footprints in the snow ... no noise of any kind. Needless to say I was late for class and on that day, I simply didn't care!

To connect with the Angel of Being, think back to a time when everything in your life was in full and complete alignment. If you don't have such memories, imagine a place where you can remove *the mask* you present to the world as your truth and *step out of your skin* for just a few moments.

Surrender Ego in all its forms and become One with Divine Source, co-creating with wisdom, love and compassion in its purest form.

Angel of Power and Glory Sandalphon

Power is often misused, abused and even misunderstood. No one willingly chooses to be powerless and yet many of us feel that we don't have the power to truly change our reality without struggle and sacrifice.

Each one of us has within us, the key to unlocking Divine Power, co-creating a reality so powerfully amazing our conscious mind cannot completely comprehend this truth. We have at our fingertips the gift of being able to harness power, transforming thought and emotion into physical form.

We are also gifted with the capability of transforming negative energy, thoughts, and emotions through the power of surrender. If we have the faith the size of a mustard seed, we can literally change our reality. Reality is a perception of truth. Truth is what we believe we can achieve.

Before we can truly begin co-creating easily, effortlessly and consistently, we must be willing to accept and own our power and live our truth. For longer than I want to admit, I have hidden from myself and the truth of who I am and what I came here to do.

We are taught to hide behind a mask, concealing truth, power and what we truly desire. In the process of coming face-to-face with all facets of our journey in physical form, we must re-learn to stand, fully transparent in the truth of who we are. Being fully and completely transparent is counter to the concept of control over all we say, do and feel. Power is the ability to reach deep within, unafraid of what others will say, think or feel about us and what we are doing with our life.

The Angel of Power and Glory, Sandalphon, will help you tap into the power of co-creation within, empowering mind, body and Spirit. To truly co-create a new, powerful reality we must be willing to walk away from everything we have come to accept as truth.

Ask Sandalphon to help you embrace your gifts and tune into the wisdom of the ages with humility and grace. With each prayer request, be open to receive. Believing with every fiber of your Being is essential in harnessing the power of co-creation in its purest form. Ask for opportunities to manifest in concrete form bringing forth all you desire into your experience, work and relationships.

Be mindful, for there can be nothing where there is even the smallest doubt … causing lack and delay. There is no one-way to receive that which you have requested and now claim as your own.

Every step forward, accepting our power is another step into the light and into the truth of who we are … whole, complete and perfect … lacking nothing.

Chapter Eight: Angels of the Cherubim

Angels of the Cherubim have been depicted as chubby, child-like Angels with tiny wings and as Lions or beasts with many eyes and wings. The image I am given is more energy and light, almost formless. Their wings glow white-hot, and they are the Celestial Record Keepers for all Sentient Beings, including humankind.

As Celestial Record Keepers, the Cherubim offer solace and strength to all who choose to be consciously awakened on their journey. We are gifted with a deep sense of knowing within, when we are attuned to and with the vibration of unconditional love.

There is no denying everything is energy and energy is everything. Within that profound statement lies the truth that all of life is intimately and intricately connected through energy.

The Cherubim are the second highest in vibration of all Nine Angelic Realms. They are able to intercede on our behalf with another when our intentions are heart-centered without ego-based agenda, surrendering the outcome.

The Angels gracing us with their presence, guidance and strength are ...
... Angel of the Word of God Gabriel
... Angel of Discernment Keruhiel
... Angel of Esoteric Wisdom Raziel
... Angel of Vision Haziel
... Angel of Knowing Asariel

These Angels are among many other Cherubim who are bearers of the Ultimate Wisdom of and within the Universe, transcending time and space as we know it. When we are centered, grounded and open to receiving guidance through wisdom and knowledge, it is the Cherubim who assist us in knowing all is in Divine Order, occurring in Divine Time. The Cherubim are all-seeing and all-knowing.

Angel of the Word of God Gabriel

The ability to tap into the wisdom and knowledge of the Universe requires us to set our human Ego-Self aside. We express all that we are through energy whether its form is thought, emotion or action. Choose your words carefully; words once spoken can never be un-said. Energy is forever circulating throughout the Universe ... positive or negative ... love or fear. Expression laced with unconditional love and compassion radiates outward. That which is given freely, without thought to agenda or outcome, returns to us tenfold.

Gabriel, Angel of the Word of God, is an expression of the Self in its purest sense. He will help you clear your Throat Chakra, which is the seat of all forms of communication. If we hold within us words of anger, hurt, frustration or fear of reprisal, we begin to store unwanted, negative energy within our physical and energy bodies. It is up to each one of us to find appropriate ways of expressing and releasing all unwanted energy.

We dis-empower our very existence when we hold on to words of anger, fear and resentment. We empower ourselves by asking Gabriel to help us dissolve all that is not ours to carry and all we wish to release. Integrity and authenticity are the cornerstones of sharing the message of your purpose with compassion.

Ask Gabriel to help you find your truth, reaching through the fear of the unknown, beyond your current comfort zone. Ask to have your Throat Chakra cleared of all that you have been holding on to and swallowing. The Angel of the Word of God will help you speak with compassion, conviction, love, truth and with complete confidence.

Self-expression is one of the most powerful and empowering ways to embrace the truth of who you are and tune into the wisdom and knowledge of the Universe.

Angel of Discernment Keruhiel

On our Spiritual Journey here on Earth, we are often faced with decisions about which way to turn, whom to trust and which decisions to make. The ability to see beyond the moment is a practiced skill. Gaining insight, tapping into past experiences and knowledge are a few of the tools we have to help us *know the truth* of any situation.

Our inner-intuitive guidance is the most reliable way to seeing clearly, making the best decision possible in any given moment. Everything we think and feel is filtered through the way or ways we perceive what's in front of us. Truth be told, we know deep within whether or not to trust what someone is saying. We know the best path to take to fulfill our purpose.

Another truth is that most of us --- including me --- simply ignore our gut feelings and intuition. Speaking for myself. one of the reasons I have ignored my own inner-warning system is because I wanted to believe what was being said or promised. When I do listen to my inner-intuitive guidance, everything always turns out for the best and I avoid challenges and obstacles. Ignoring our intuitive nudges causes stress and tension.

The Angel of Discernment, Keruhiel, is an incredibly powerful Angel who will help you see past what's said or shown to you. His robes are brilliant violet-red and when he speaks his words are laced with flames to burn through illusion, clearing the way for truth, love and light.

Keruhiel will help you know the truth of any situation so you are always being shown the truth. It is our responsibility to trust what is being shown and given to us. Sometimes we choose the path of least resistance rather than take appropriate action or non-action depending on the guidance we receive in that moment.

Ask the Angel of Discernment for strength and courage to follow his guidance, trusting that the outcome is for your highest and best good. For example, we know when agreeing to a contract, hiring someone or beginning a relationship if it's in our best interest or it seems too good to be true. The best way to take advantage of Keruhiel's guidance is to ask before making a major decision.

Ask for help to make a new, *better for you* decision when you know it is time to move forward in another direction. Be willing to admit to yourself that you made a mistake, choose to make a new decision and move on. Decisions we find ourselves faced with making and following through with, are not always popular. Sometimes you'll be met with resistance from others. Ultimately you need to do what's best for you.

Keruhiel is nudging me to remind us all to ground ourselves and come from our heart-center and not Ego when making decisions that affect others.

Each time you ask for guidance, you open yourself to receiving what you have asked for ... trust and act on that which is given. It will get easier to see past surface appearances with insight and wisdom and with practice.

Angel of Esoteric Wisdom Raziel

Every experience, relationship, success and failure, gifts us with knowledge. When we tap into our vast resources, we're able to navigate our path with grace, laced with wisdom. We are the sum of all things learned, discovered, accepted and even what we have rejected and resisted along the way. Wisdom is the gift of recognizing the difference between truth and illusion. It is about knowing when to take a *Leap of Faith* and when to take a step back, weighing all options.

Esoteric Wisdom, from my perspective, is the ability to connect with our Higher-Self, Angels and Spirit, and seeking truth in the absence of Ego-chitter chatter. It's also knowledge beyond physical perception, which is intangible. Esoteric Wisdom is something that is sensed or felt, often without a way to validate or confirm what is received.

Raziel, Angel of Esoteric Wisdom, helps us release false beliefs that prevent us from seeing and recognizing truth from illusion. He also helps us rise above the ordinary, everyday negative experiences which taint and lower our inner-vibration. A problem, challenge or obstacle cannot be solved at the same level of vibration in which it was created. We must rise above what is in front of us to see the solution.

Ask Raziel to help you heal the past and to experience balance and harmony in this present moment. Wisdom is recognizing a belief or pattern of behavior that does not serve you, your purpose or your Spiritual Path. Being willing to see a challenge or obstacle from a different perspective is the key to tapping into your inner-wisdom.

You can ask Raziel to help you reach past surface beliefs and Ego-chitter chatter that prevents you from truly moving forward towards your dream of fulfilling your life-purpose. Each time you willingly tap into wisdom, you empower you to take that next step along your pathway with confidence.

When you get to the edge of what you know, you'll find what used to work, no longer does. Being willing to be willing to show-up more powerfully is facing yourself with unconditional love and wisdom.

Angel of Vision Haziel

The ability to see beyond the present moment and current reality is essential to raising our inner-vibration, connecting with our Higher-Self. What is it that you see when you look into the mirror of truth? Are you willing to see below the outer-layers of your physical body and what your Ego is showing you to be reality? I have recently begun to go deeper within, embracing the shadows of past hurts in an effort to completely free myself and my vision.

For some, when they hear the word *vision*, they think of having visions of what is "yet" to come. Others see through layers of energy, accessing information, messages and images that contain golden nuggets of truth in their purest form. Being able to see the objects of your desire in as much detail as possible within your inner-sight, your imagination, speeds up the manifestation process tenfold. The ability to hold fast to the image we create without fear and doubt deepens our emotional and mental connection to what we desire.

It isn't always easy to imagine a particular goal. Instead of trying to come up with the *perfect* image or images, ask Haziel, Angel of Vision, to help you keep things simple.

To manifest prosperity, some of my clients like to visualize golden coins piling up around them. Others imagine a specific number of people showing up for a live event. Still others imagine what it will feel like to manifest their dreams and life their purpose in prosperity and abundance. You can imagine the kind of house or relationship you want to have. I have used my imagination to heal my relationships with my parents by *seeing* them in a bubble of rose light.

Haziel has just given me her colors, which are rose and deep amethyst purple. Rose as you may already know symbolizes unconditional love. Amethyst purple is associated with healing and Spirituality, connecting us with Spirit and Angels. Ask the Angel of Vision to help you clear your mind and your heart of anything that attempts to distract you from *seeing* the object of your desire clearly and effortlessly.

Focus all your energy, thoughts and emotions to manifest your vision into reality in physical form. Haziel reminds us to focus on our vision for at least 5 minutes every day. Where our attention goes, energy flows. Thoughts feed emotion. Emotions stir thoughts. Are you feeding positive or negative emotions into your vision?

There is a *space* or *zone* of energy that is created each time we are co-creating with Haziel and all Angels. The only words I have to describe this *energy zone*, is a deep sense of peaceful knowing. In this space, there is only trust and faith, crystal clarity and a sense of knowing that the vision of your heart's desire is simply transitioning from the Realm of Spirit into concrete shape in your life and experience.

Angel of Knowing Asariel

One of the four intuitive gifts or skills is claircognizance, *an unwavering sense of knowing* something to be a truth.
Examples of *knowing* something to be a truth ...
... energy healing working sight unseen
... sensing energy through email or text messages
... sensing an intention or agenda behind words spoken or written
... channeling this book

Have you ever experienced a time when you felt energy or received an intuitive thought when you were completely focused on something or someone else? Or perhaps you felt the presence of Spirit or Angels around you ... or an idea just popped into your head and *you just knew* it was the answer to a question or solution to a problem you were wanting to solve.

The Angel of Knowing, Asariel, is beckoning you with open arms, ready to help you become consciously aware of your ...

... surroundings
... emotions
... thoughts
... inner-vibration
... inner-intuitive guidance

Asariel asks us to begin trusting what we receive with a deeper awareness, taking time to accept what we are given. There is a way to discern the difference between what is being given to us through Asariel and Angels and what is being generated by Ego-chitter chatter.

The next time you *know* something, whatever that is for you, take a moment or two to notice where you felt this knowing collect in your physical body? For most people this resonance or *knowing energy* manifests in their Heart-center of Solar Plexus. It will usually be one or the other. This means, the more you are aware of *where* in your body the *physical sensation of knowing* occurs, the easier it is for you to trust the messages or guidance you are receiving.

The Angel of Knowing encourages us to open our mind and heart, expanding our conscious awareness as we travel our Spiritual Path. Knowing is a sense of absolute certainty that a decision we are about to make is right and perfect for us. Asariel is handing us the keys to Universal Knowing for the asking. We must ask and then be open to receive.

Because we are taught something must be tangible --- seen heard, tasted or touched physically --- we often discount what we pick-up energetically. The more we are consciously aware of what is happening within and around us, the more we are tuned in to the vibrations of the Universe, our inner-intuitive self and the Angelic Realm.

Chapter Nine: Angels of the Seraphim

The Seraphim are the highest and most Divinely Radiant of all Angels. Angels of this Angelic Realm are Celestial Beings of Bright White Light, representing the very Essence of Creation itself. Because these Angels of Unconditional Love and Creation vibrate at the highest levels, they are also known as the Burning Ones.

At the highest levels of Creation, the Seraphim are overseers, shapers, makers and preservers of the Essence of Oneness in its purest, most holy form we humans are able to understand and comprehend. As creators and originators of miracles, these Angels encourage and support our inner Spiritual Expansion as we discover and explore our path.

As I close my eyes to better receive the image the Seraphim want me to share with you, I *see* massive gleaming, fiery white chariots pulled by equally massive, winged horses. Each Angel of this Realm has 4 faces, enabling them to face each of the four cardinal directions simultaneously. They have 3 pairs of wings, symbolizing Eternal Love, Essence of Love and the very Miracle of Love.

This may just be the most difficult of all lessons we humans and to learn and accept as truth. That is the lesson of love, unconditional love as a truth rather than a mere theory that is seemingly out of reach and unattainable. When we are in a *space of love* emotionally, mentally and energetically, we are at peace no matter what appears to be happening or not happening around us in our physical world.

Just prior to the writing of this chapter, I truly had lost my way. My world as I knew it suddenly came crashing down around me. There was a period of twelve plus days that were a downward spiral into the blackest Dark Night of the Soul I have ever encountered. It was a metamorphosis of death and rebirth and transcendence.

Connecting and working with the Seraphim now, following my death and re-birth, isn't really a surprise because I now have a deeper, more humble understanding of the illusion of separation and loss of Oneness with my inner-self, my Soul and that of Divine Source and my beloved Angels. The Seraphim

Angels of Love, Light and Fire offer you and me the gift of reconciliation through unconditional love.

The four Angels who are here to accompany us as we journey through this Angelic Realm of the most holy, extending a helping hand and hearts, overflowing with unconditional love are ...

... Angel Chief of the Seraphim Jeho'el
... Angel of the Essence of Love Sama'el
... Angel of the Miracle of Love Seraphi'el
... Angel of Eternal Love Uriel

There are only two emotions ---love or fear --- which show-up in our human experience as ...
... truth or illusion
... peace or chaos
... forgiveness or resentment
... prosperity or lack
... infinite possibilities or limitation
... surrender of resistance

How we choose to walk our path is entirely up to us. As easy as it is to write these words, I am keenly aware we must first wipe clear all previous fear-based programming with forgiveness and unconditional love, healing the illusion of separation.

Angel Chief of the Seraphim Jeho'el

Healing the Illusion of Separation is perhaps one of the most difficult and challenging lessons of conscious awareness we will ever encounter. If love is the most powerful of all emotions, why then does it feel and look like fear is and has the most power? That is a question I have *asked* so many times I have literally lost count! The answer feels simplistic and yet, its truth cannot be denied.

Fear feeds doubt, lack and limitation. We are taught to fear strangers, our intuition and the unknown. It causes chaos and confusion, mistrust and dis-ease. Negativity in any form preys on our feelings of being unworthy and undeserving of what is already ours in Spirit. All that is being asked of us is to be open and willing to accept one of the most sacred truths ...

that we are One with Divine Source and we are always connected, never separated except by thought and emotion.

The sole mission or purpose of Jeho'el, Angel Chief of the Seraphim, is to oversee all Angels, in all Realms and help us see beyond ourselves. Jeho'el serves as the bearer of the Light and the Way through the shadows of fear and doubt and into the Light of Love. His robes are amethyst purple, the vibration of healing, trust and faith and Oneness with the Divine.

This Divinely masculine Angel's head is surrounded with a turbine like, Rainbow Light symbolizing the physical journey up through our Chakra energy centers ... and ... the blending of the Earthly Plane of Existence and the Realm of Spirit. This Angel will help us remember the truth of our own Divinity, the truth of being created with and through the power of unconditional love in its purest, most holy form.

The Angel Chief of the Seraphim asks us to give to him, all fears of being unlovable, being unworthy and underserving of experiencing the promises of Divine Oneness, balancing our having a physical body and being Spiritual. Close your eyes and breathe deeply. Imagine Jeho'el is standing in front of you with cupped hands, waiting for you to give all your Earthly cares and worries to him. His shoulders are broad, his heart completely open, pouring forth unconditional love and acceptance of all that you now give to him for healing and transmutation, in this most Sacred of Moments. His wings gently enfold you, allowing you to simply let go of all that truly no longer serves you.

Ask Jeho'el to help you find the courage and inner-strength to surrender unto him all past pain and sorrow that has kept the illusion of separateness alive within your heart and mind. Allow your body to purge all negative energy and simply let go. Just let go, let it all go.

In truth, there is no separation, there is only Oneness. Face the North, the point of origin and know the truth ... as co-creators, we have been gifted with dominion over the thoughts and emotions we entertain through our human-self and Ego-chitter chatter.

Keep what you must; knowing as with all things, there is a cost to holding on to that which serves you not. Instead, choose light, love and fire. Choose *Light* to see the way. Choose *Love* to follow your path. Choose *Fire* to burn off and purify.

The gift of re-connecting with the Sacred Truth of Oneness is total and complete alignment, a sense of knowing we are loved beyond measure.

Angel of the Essence of Love Sama'el

At the very core of all that we are, is love, unconditional love. It is elusive. It is something we all crave to receive and experience. Yet, most of us are simply clueless as to what unconditional love is or how to give it. To express love without conditions, strings attached or a hidden agenda, is not what most of us are taught or have experienced. There is a misconception that to love unconditionally, gives others permission to violate our boundaries or take advantage of our openness. Nothing could be farther from the truth!

Unconditional love has been explained to me as first honoring the Self, honoring others as you wish to be honored. It is identified as non-judgment and honoring the choices we make in an effort to live a life of prosperity, contentment and living our purpose fully.

The Angel of the Essence of Love, Sama'el, helps us go deep within, below the surface of Ego-chitter chatter, connecting with our true nature of Love and Light. Love is the purest expression of our true nature. We are either projecting love or fear. It is that simple and that complicated, all in the same moment. When fear is present, love is absent. When love is present, fear is non-existent.

If you truly desire to live a love-filled life, Sama'el will be by your side 24/7 as you begin such an arduous journey of self-reflection, healing, purging and eventual transcendence. We must be willing to face our inner-demons with courage and persistence, which have shown-up in our experiences along the way.

The Angel of the Essence of Love helps us identify, heal and eliminate deep-seated beliefs that cause us to withhold love, even from ourselves.

We have learned and practiced ways of ...
... devaluing and discounting our self-worth

... being undeserving of living a prosperous life, fulfilling our purpose

... judging and allowing the judgment of others to dictate our actions

Ask Sama'el for protection as you journey inward, re-discovering and re-connecting with your inner-knowing that you are love and loved beyond your understanding. Ask to shed all pre-conceived ideas and all experiences ---past and present --- that are not of love. Sama'el will be by your side, guiding your every step, shielding you from negative energy.

Face the East, the symbol of new beginnings ... the rising of the limitless potential and opportunities. Walking the path of unconditional love and non-judgment is not easy. It requires courage and persistence and a commitment to yourself that will stretch you beyond anything you have ever experienced before.

Make no mistake; Ego-chitter chatter will raise its voice, making you question your own sanity. It will cause you to want to shrink back from the edge and do its best to talk you out of taking that Leap of Faith. The higher we climb energetically and the farther we are willing to travel along our chosen path, the easier and more challenging it will become.

It is not always easy balancing a Spiritual Path and an Earthly life. Perseverance and patience, self-care and compassion are the secrets to melting all forms of resistance.

Angel of the Miracle of Love Seraphi'el

The journey during the channeling of this book has been filled with many twists and turns, peaks and valleys, darkness, shadow and light. As I *settle* my human-self, grounding, connecting and opening to receive what Seraphi'el has to share with us, I am guided to share a story with you ... there are no accidents or coincidences, only that which co-incides one with the other.

A few hours before connecting with and channeling Seraphi'el, I was feeling quite overwhelmed with the transition my life and work are currently experiencing in this moment. After a few minutes of deep breathing, I felt calmer and thought the feeling of being overwhelmed had completely dissipated. A little while later, even though I was still feeling calm and relatively peaceful, tears started spilling down my face.

The trigger was sharing an experience with my dear friend and long-time accountability partner. At that moment, I stopped and allowed me to feel what I was feeling. I *asked* my Angels to help me surrender the fear and to the transition process itself. I know the truth even when Ego-chitter chatter raises its voice of lack and limitation, which often trigger feelings of being all-alone, being a failure, unlovable and at times simply invisible.

The Angel of the Miracle of Love, Seraphi'el, is here with me, showering me with so much love and comfort, I feel a bit light-headed. All any of us --- including me --- need to do is *ask* and be open to receive what we have asked for. Yes, it does require us to let go of pre-conceived ideas of not being worthy or special enough to connect with Seraphi'el or any other Angel.

Seraphi'el has the face or faces of an Angel and the body of a great Eagle. An Eagle symbolized soaring high above the ordinary, seeing great distances ... and ... being able to focus with laser-like precision. Through the Miracle of Love --- unconditional love and acceptance --- we are capable of spreading our wings, knowing we are supported each and every step of the way.

Love is surrendering all doubt, and all that truly has never served you, your work or your purpose. It is also about forgiveness and healing, letting go and clearing space mentally, emotionally and energetically to receive the gift of contentment and peace of mind.

Ask Seraphi'el to place her left hand over your heart-center and her right hand behind your heart-center on your back. Breathe deeply seven times, close your eyes and imagine or sense energy flowing in and out through your heart-center. I am being given the image that this is a circulation cleansing, clearing and purifying the energy that flows into your heart and then flows outward into every cell of your physical body.

As the Sun sets in the West, Seraphi'el asks us to purge all thought and emotion at the end of our day, giving us an opportunity to renew our energy during our sleep time. When we are in a state of love, we are consciously connected with

Divine Source and we are unaffected by the physical world because our inner-vibration is love.

Coming from and being mindful of love, can become second-nature to us without having to think about it. Unconditional love is the origin of our truth … without all the filters and negative energy walls that we have built and reinforced to protect ourselves, we return to a conscious presence of the Miracle of Love.

Angel of Eternal Love Uriel

The word *eternal* feels a little beyond my comprehension in terms of eternal love because there's no point of reference in this physical world of substance and matter. My understanding, in this moment, about this concept is this … *eternal* is having no beginning and no end which feels and is counter-intuitive … the exact polar opposite of what life in physical form appears to show us.

To everything there is a cycle of birth and eventual death. So then, how can we have a sense of understanding … an inner-knowing about that which is nerver ending? So, I've been *asking* Uriel, the Angel of Eternal Love, to help me first understand this concept and then be able to clearly share it with you. There's a smile on my face in the example he gave me.

Think of something --- an experience or situation --- that triggered fear of the future, or a relationship issue that had your insides all twisted in knots. This is a perfect scenario for Ego-chitter chatter to start one of its endless loops of negative *"whoa is me"* or whatever else it *throws-up* at us. It's like those thoughts and feelings have always been a part of us and will never-ever go away!

Okay – now, turn that around and imagine this scenario … in a circle all around you are Angels. You are in the center of this circle and the only thing you feel is love, acceptance, support, healing and compassion. In other words … all you feel and / or sense is an outpouring of contentment, pure joy, and harmony … continuous, unconditional love!

All that is being asked of us is to be willing to suspend all fear of this being a trick or yet another deception designed to lure us into a false sense of hope that we are lovable, treasured and of value ... that our life in physical form actually has meaning. And that our purpose is truly born of love, through love for love of Divine Source and our existence here in this Realm.

Uriel, the Angel of Eternal Love is also the Angel who helps us manifest our deepest desires. Think about it ... in those moments when you are in complete alignment --- mentally, emotionally, energetically and Spiritually --- situations resolve themselves and opportunities appear as if out of thin air.

Thin air is the stretching or thinning of the veil between the Realm of Sprit and our realm of dense physical energy. *Thin air* is a stretching or parting of energy allowing what is already ours in the Realm of Spirit to manifest into our experience in physical form. Now that --- in my humble opinion --- is both magical and mystical!

One of the ways we can *create thin air space* is to *enter the Silence,* allowing us to re-connect with the truth of Eternal Love deep within our Soul. Ask Uriel to show you the way past disbelief of being loveable and loved, melting resistance to receiving that which is already yours in heart, mind and Spirit.

The Angel of Eternal Love will help you see past the learned fear of conditional and limited love. You don't have to be someone or something different. You do get to accept you as you are ... warts, scrapes, dings and scars ... just the way you are right now.

The last of the four cardinal directions, South, symbolizes the vessel of receiving our good with an open mind and an open heart. We are either rooted in love or fear. There is no in-between. In love, we experience a deep knowing that all our Earthly needs are provided for even when the "how" has not yet been revealed to us.

This is a truth I practice every single day, throughout my day with conscious awareness. Admittedly, I haven't been able, until now, to truly access and experience a sense of eternal love. Another truth is ... there are "moments" that pop-up to remind me how *fragile balance* can actually be if I am not mindful of all the good in my life right now in this moment.

In Closing ...

Right now in this moment, I have no clue how this book is going to be completed; edited, proof-read and ready for release by the end of November, 2015 ... *I just know it is.*

Less than 120 days ago (it is now November 24, 2015), the laptop I used for several years completely crashed, taking with it the draft of this book. Everything that has been shared with you in these pages was channeled through every Angel that graces us with their presence, guidance and loving words filled with healing and compassion. Thankfully, two-thirds of our work – the Angels and mine --- was recoverable. Every word was been written out by-hand in a notebook while sitting in my favorite coffee shop.

The channeling of this book --- Sacred Angel Realms --- began as everything else does ... through guidance. After I received guidance to be the vessel for this book, it would be another 8 months before I almost felt ready to start! You see, there wasn't very much information on any of the Angelic Realms, just a few scattered paragraphs on the internet and in a few books.

Hence the persistent nudges by Angels to write their story. Some would say that the writing of this book was easy because I talk with Angels every day and only took eighteen-months to complete. In reality, this is or has been a life-time in the creating. The first two chapters were relatively easy because I was most familiar with Guardian Angels and Archangels.

Some days I was only able to channel one section of a chapter in a single-sitting. Other times I could channel as many as four sections in a single-channeling session. Each step of the way, I had or got to raise my own vibration so I could connect at higher and higher levels of vibration to receive the information that is being shared with you in these pages.

In the beginning, I naively thought this book could be channeled and written in as little as nine months. Little did I know the journey that would unfold within each of the Angelic Realms ... it's best that I didn't have a clue about the inner-growth and expansion that I was about to undertake. I might not have ever gotten started.

There is information within these pages that, more than likely, will not be found anywhere else … there were times I questioned what was being written. Sentences were erased only to "re-appear" word-for-word … sometimes more than once.

Hopefully you have enjoyed this book as much as I have enjoyed being the vessel and the channel for Angels and you! It has truly been a labor of love, surrender, healing and transformation for me … and … I, hope for you too. Transformation is the only way we are truly able to walk our Spiritual Path.

Here's to you and your Spiritual Path, may it be everything and more than you ever hoped and dreamed it could or would be!

Much Love, Light, Peace and Prosperity,
Angel Lady Terrie Marie, D.Ms.

PS … I would LOVE to hear from you, your thoughts and how this book --- if it has --- impacted your life and the way you are now able to connect with Angels. You can email me directly at TerrieMarie@AngelDreamTeam.com

Resources

Bletzer, June G Ph.D.: The Encyclopedic Psychic Dictionary; New Leaf Distributing Company. Lithia Springs, Georgia; 1986

Davidson, Gustav: A Dictionary of Angels including the fallen angels; The Free Press; New Your, NY; 1967

Wauters, Ambika: The Angel Oracle Working with the Angels for Guidance, Inspiration and Love; St. Martin's Press; New York; 1995

Webster, Richard; Encyclopedia of Angels; Llewelyn Publications; Woodbury, Minnesota; 2009

Angel Dream Team Cards; Angel Lady Terrie Marie, D.Ms.; Angel Lady Aurora, LLC Publications; El Paso, Texas; 2013

About the Author

Terrie Marie, D.Ms., also known as the Angel Whisperer, has an **Unusual and Highly Effective** way of showing Heart-Centered Women and Men how to show-up more powerfully in their life, work and business when they access their Ultimate Angel Dream Team.

Angel Lady Terrie Marie **specializes in showing her clients how to directly access and receive Divine Guidance through their Higher-Self and Angels**, raise your inner-vibration, your Divine Wealth Frequency, change thought patterns, enhance the Law of Attraction and magnify your manifesting power.

She helps you **discover, explore and learn practical, easy-to-use techniques**, tips and tools to increase prosperity and abundance with more harmony and less stress. The Angel Lady shows you how to **trust your intuition and gut feelings** with a heightened sense of empowerment and confidence.

Her subtle, **powerful insights create life-changing transformations from the inside out.** Terrie Marie has helped Heart and Soul-Centered women and men in Australia, South Africa, Ghana, New Zealand, Germany, Belgium, Canada, United Kingdom, Mexico, Brazil, Sweden and the United States.

Terrie Marie, D.Ms. has the unique ability to **connect and communicate with Angels** which makes her a highly sought after Angel Mentor and Angel Whisperer.

When the Angel Lady is being interviewed or speaking to International audiences, her **high energy ignites the atmosphere with her empowering message**, her unconditional love shines bright and intuitive insights flow through her. She creates Sacred Space to ***transform goals and dreams into reality.***

Connect with Angel Lady Terrie Marie, D.Ms.

ANGEL DREAM TEAM

http://www.angeldreamteam.com/

FREE GIFTS

Divine Wealth MindMap:
https://angellady.leadpages.co/divinewealth/

Dissolve Negative Energy: https://angellady.leadpages.net/free-report-negative-energy/

Angels of Prosperity Video Course:
https://angellady.leadpages.net/prosperity-angels-opt-in/

BLOG

http://www.angeldreamteam.com/blog

FACEBOOK

https://www.facebook.com/AngelDreamTeam/

YOUTUBE

https://www.youtube.com/channel/UC2TOHSWJ53K4fDD_bM9H-xg

TWITTER

https://twitter.com/AngelLadyTM

LINKEDIN

https://www.linkedin.com/in/angelladytm

www.ingramcontent.com/pod-product-compliance
Lightning Source LLC
LaVergne TN
LVHW020936090426
835512LV00020B/3381